Tipawan Thampusana

Thai for English Speaking Learners

Grammatical and cultural approaches

Editions Duang Kamol

1995 by Tipawan Thampusana - Matthias S.W. Abold.
All rights reserved

Published by:
   Editions Duang Kamol
   G.P.O.Box 427
   Bangkok 10501 Thailand
      Publisher's No. 2/1995 February - 2,000 copies

Printed in Thailand by:
   D.K. Printing House, Ltd.
   205/54-57 Ngamwongwan Rd.
   Bangkok 10210

Distributors:
   Book Wholesales House (Thailand) Ltd.
   90/21-25 Rajaprarob Rd.
   Makkasan Bangkok 10400
   Tel. 245-5586, 247-1030   Fax: 247-1033

ISBN 974-210-5669

To

Matthias S. W. Abold

Preface

As a native who studied Thai and Non Formal Education for Bachelor and Master degrees respectively, I have had chances in teaching both country fellows and foreigners our language for a few years.

The lack of grammatical learning materials for Thai as a foreign language prompted me to prepare all lessons for my foreign learners myself. The materials have been through years of experiences tried out and always improved.

As a native, I am much appreciated when foreigners are interested in our language. As a teacher and author, I hope that my effort can, at least at a level, help the learners to get a good start with a new learning experience.

Any opinion, advice and criticism are always warmly welcome.

Tipawan Thampusana-Abold
(Author)

Contents

		Page
Getting to Know Your Learning Materials		9
Lesson I	พยัญชนะ (Consonants)	13
Lesson II	สระ (Vowels)	23
	- การแนะนำตนเอง (Self Introduction)	28
Lesson III	วรรณยุกต์ (Tones)	33
Lesson IV	History and Main Characteristics of Thai Language	37
Lesson V	Special Rules for Vowels	47
Lesson V.I	Exercises for Vowel - ะ	55
	- แล้วคุณล่ะ (And You?)	57
	- กำลัง (Doing)	57
	- จะ (Will do)	57
	- การทักทาย (Greeting)	58
Lesson V.II	Exercises for Vowel เ - ะ	63
	- นี่ภาษาไทยเรียกว่าอะไร (How Do You Call It in Thai?)	64
	- การแนะนำผู้อื่น (Introducing Other People)	65
	- สัปดาห์ (Week)	65
	- เรื่องของโทนี่ (The Story of Tony)	65

Lesson V.III Exercises for Vowel แ - ะ 71

- ขอบคุณและไม่เป็นไร (Thank You and You Are Welcome)...... 72
- ทำไม (Why...?) 72
- เรื่องของน้ำตาล (The Story of Namtan) 73
- The Word ให้ 74

Lesson V.IV Exercises for Vowel เ - อ 79

- คุณเรียนภาษาไทยมานานแล้วหรือ 79
  (Have You Already Learned Thai for Long?)
- ขอโทษและไม่เป็นไร (Excuse Me and That's Alright) 80
- เสียใจและขอบคุณ (I'm Sorry and Thank You) 81
- The Word เสีย 82

Lesson V.V Exercises for Vowel โ - ะ 85

- ครอบครัวไทย (The Thai Family) 86
- วันเกิดของคุณย่า (Grandma's Birthday)........................... 91

Lesson V.VI Exercises for Vowels - อ and ั ว 95

- อักษรควบกล้ำ (Double Initials) 96
- ปีและเดือน (Year and Month) 98
- การแสดงความคิดเห็นและความรู้สึก 98
  (Expressing Opinions and Feelings)

Lesson VI กฎการผันเสียงวรรณยุกต์ (Rules of Tones) 105

Lesson VII อักษรนำ (Leading Consonants) 111

- การขอร้อง (Request) 113
- การเปรียบเทียบ (Comparison) 115

Lesson VIII	สรรพนามและนาม (Pronoun and Noun)	123
Lesson IX	ประโยค (Sentence)	133
	- The Word ก็	137
Lesson X	คำถามและคำตอบ (Question and Answer)	141
Lesson XI	คำสั่ง (Imperative)	147
	- การปฏิเสธ (Negation)	148
	- กรรมวาจก (Passive Voice)	151
Lesson XII	การนับ เวลา และวันที่ (Counting, Time, and Date)	155
Lesson XIII	Additional Grammar Rules	159
	- ใ- หรือ ไ- (Rules for ใ- or ไ-)	159
	- ๆ (Rules for ๆ)	160
	- The words เป็น, มี, มา, ไป, เพื่อ, เล่น, ถือ, ได้, พอ	161
Lesson XVI	จดหมาย (Letter)	167
Appendix	Useful Dialogues with Related Information on Various Themes	175

Getting to Know Your Learning Materials

The learning materials comprise of a textbook with exercises, vocabulary lists, keys (with the sign ☑) to the exercises, and a cassette.

In Thai language, consonants and vowels are separated into 2 different groups of alphabets. There are 44 **consonants** (2 hereof are not in use anymore) which have **21 sounds as initials** and **8 as finals of syllables**. The vowels consist of 32. Not all of the consonants and vowels' sounds can be compared with those of English or any other Latin-related languages.

Hence, phonetic transcription is not used in this book. **The cassette is absolutely needed**, especially for the very first lessons, in order that you can practise the right pronunciation since the beginning. The sign ⊛ tells you where you need to work with the cassette.

Thailand, like other countries, has dialects. The language used in the book and cassette is **Bangkok Thai** which is standard and official. Every Thai, no matter from which region, can understand it and the Thai usually, due to the centralized school system, speak this official language with foreigners.

The book contains not only grammar points but also cultural aspects of Thai life. Your will and effort to learn with the help of the materials will step by step provide you capability in reading, writing, speaking, and listening - the four skills which anyone wishing to master a language should develop at the same time.

The assignments for exercises have English translation at the beginning but as soon as you are expected, thanks to the knowledge you should have got by then, to be able to read and understand them yourself - the translation will be no more available.

In the vocabulary lists at the end of each lesson, meanings and some grammar points are given. In some lessons needed additional vocabularies are prepared to give you assistance while working on the exercises or to help expanding your knowledge. Some vocabularies appear several times through the whole book but they will be only once at the first time in the lists. So **an additional good dictionary is highly recommended.**

These abbreviations will be used for grammatical terms:

ส.	- สรรพนาม	Pronoun
น.	- คำนาม	Noun
ก.	- กริยา	Verb
ค.	- คุณศัพท์	Adjective
ว.	- วิเศษณ์	Adverb
บ.	- บุพบท	Preposition
สัน.	- สันธาน	Conjunction

Please keep in mind that the grammatical structure of Thai language is completely different from any of Latin-related languages. Thus, the words' functions are also different. For example อาจจะ (perhaps) in Thai is a helping verb whereas it is in English an adverb, etc....

Lesson I

พยัญชนะ Consonants

Thai language has 44 consonants but 2 among them are no more in use. The 42 current consonants have 21 sounds as initials and 8 as finals. So there are several consonants which have exactly the same sounds and tones. Hence, the names of the consonants can help decreasing confusion. For example: both ค and ฆ have the sound of **KO** with the middle tone. To know for sure which one is needed in a word, one must ask if it is ค ควาย (KO KWAI) or ฆ ระฆัง (KO RAKANG).

To pronounce Thai consonants, the vowel อ (like in floor) is used. For example: ก is pronounced กอ (GO) .....

Now you can practise writing Thai consonants. Please start and follow the arrows.

Consonants and their Pronunciation	Names of Consonants and their Pronunciation		Meaning of the Names
ก GO	ไก่	GAI	chicken
ข KO	ไข่	KAI	egg
ค KO	ควาย	KWAI	water buffalo
ฆ KO	ระฆัง	RAKANG	bell
ง NGO	งู	NGU	snake
จ JO	จาน	JAN	dish
ฉ SHO	ฉิ่ง	SHING	small cup-shaped cymbals

ช	SHO	ช้าง	SHANG	elephant
ซ	SO	โซ่	SOO	chain
ฌ	SHO	เฌอ	SHER	tree
ญ	YO	หญิง	YING	woman, girl, female
ฎ	DO	ชฎา	SHADA	crown
ฏ	DTO	ปฏัก	BPADTAK	spear
ฐ	TO	ฐาน	TAN	base
ฑ	TO	มณโฑ	MOONTOO	Moontoo (name)

ฌ	TO	ผู้เฒ่า	PUTAU	elderly people
ณ	NO	เณร	NEN	Buddhist novice
ด	DO	เด็ก	DEK	child
ต	DTO	เต่า	DTAU	turtle
ถ	TO	ถุง	TUNG	bag
ท	TO	ทหาร	TAHAN	soldier
ธ	TO	ธง	TOONG	flag
น	NO	หนู	NU	mouse

บ	BO	ใบไม้	BAIMAI	leaf
ป	BPO	ปลา	BPLA	fish
ผ	PO	ผึ้ง	PEUNG	bee
ฝ	FO	ฝา	FA	lid
พ	PO	พาน	PAN	tray
ฟ	FO	ฟัน	FAN	tooth
ภ	PO	สำเภา	SAMPAU	sailing ship
ม	MO	ม้า	MA	horse

ย	YO	ยักษ์	YAK	giant
ร	RO	เรือ	REU-A	boat
ล	LO	ลิง	LING	monkey
ว	WO	แหวน	WAEN	ring
ศ	SO	ศาลา	SALA	pavilion
ษ	SO	ฤษี	REUSI	ascetic
ส	SO	เสือ	SEU-A	tiger
ห	HO	หีบ	HIB	box, chest

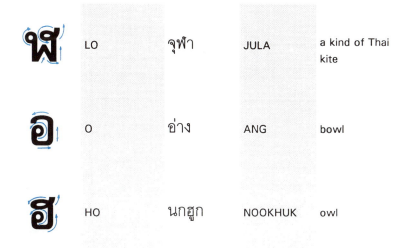

Thai is a tonal language. This means a mere tone can change the meaning of a word.

However, there are only 2 basic tones of all consonants, when they stand alone:

- the middle tone, like in the word "land"
- the rising tone, like the end of a question which starts with a helping verb.

The consonants with rising basic tone are on the following table printed in italics, such as ฉ ษ etc.

42 consonants	เสียง (SOUND)					
	21 as initials			8 as finals		
ก	Go	G	กาน	Look	K	กาก
ข ค ฆ	Keep	K	ขาน คาน		K	กาค
ง	---	NG	งาน	RiNG	NG	กาง
จ	Jane	J	จาน	RaT	T	กาจ
ฉ ช ฌ	She	SH	ฉาน ชาน		T	กาช
ฎ ฑ	Do	D	ดาน		T	กาด
ฏ ฏ	---	DT	ตาน		T	กาต
ฐ ถ ท ธ ฒ ฑ	To	T	ถาน ทาน		T	กาท
น ณ	Nun	N	นาน	NuN	N	กาน
บ	Bob	B	บาน	ToP	P	กาบ
ป	---	BP	ปาน		P	กาป
ผ พ ภ	Pond	P	ผาน พาน		P	กาพ
ฟ ฝ	Fan	F	ฟาน ฝาน		P	กาฟ
ม	Mom	M	มาน	MoM	M	กาม
ร	Rose	R	ราน	NuN	N	การ
ล ฬ	Love	L	ลาน		N	กาล
ย	Yes	Y	ยาน	THAI	:::I	กาย
ญ	Yes	Y	ญาน	NuN	N	กาญ
ว	Wide	W	วาน	FaUna	:::U	กาว
ซ ส ศ ษ	Sand	S	ซาน สาน	RaT	T	กาส
ห ฮ	Head	H	หาน ฮาน		---	
อ	depends on its vowel.				---	

The 42 consonants are divided into 3 groups:
(This separation will be needed in some later lessons!)

อักษรสูง (high consonants): 10
The basic tone of this group is the **rising tone**.

ข ฉ ฐ ถ ผ ฝ ส ศ ษ ห

อักษรกลาง (middle consonants): 9
The basic tone of this group is the **middle tone**.

ก จ ด ฎ ต ฏ บ ป อ

อักษรต่ำ (low consonants): 23
The basic tone of this group is the **middle tone**. The low consonants are further divided into 2 groups.

❶ **อักษรเดี่ยว** (single consonants): 10

ง ญ ณ น ม ย ร ล ว ฬ

❷ **อักษรคู่** (twin consonants): 13

ค ฅ ช ซ ฌ ฑ ฒ ท ธ พ ฟ ภ ฮ

แบบฝึกหัดการฟัง (Listening exercise):
From each pair of consonants you will hear one sound, point them out.

ก	ด	ง	น	จ	ช	ฉ	ซ
ด	ต	ท	ถ	อ	ฮ	ล	ร
พ	ผ	ฝ	ฟ	ม	น	บ	ป

แบบฝึกหัดการออกเสียง (Pronunciation exercise):

Pronounce the following consonants, then check with the cassette. If it is not really correct, try once again.

ด   ง   ก   น   ย   ช   ถ   ภ   ส   ว   ฟ   ล   พ   ข   ม

แบบฝึกหัดการเขียน (Writing exercise):

Practise writing each consonants until you can do it without the models.

Vocabulary:

น.	พยัญชนะ	-	consonant
น.	ควาย	-	water buffalo
น.	ระฆัง	-	bell
น.	เสียง	-	sound, voice
น.	อักษร	-	consonant
ค.,ว.	สูง	-	high, tall
ค.,ว.	กลาง	-	middle
ค.,ว.	ต่ำ	-	low
ค.,ว.	เดี่ยว	-	single, alone
ค.,ว.	คู่	-	twin, double
น.	แบบฝึกหัด	-	exercise
น.	การ	-	prefix to help making nouns out of verbs or other nouns
ก.	ฟัง	-	listen
ก.	ออกเสียง	-	pronounce
ก.	เขียน	-	write

 Listening exercise

ด   ง   จ   ช   ต   ถ   อ   ร   ผ   ฟ   ม   ป

Lesson II

สระ Vowels

There are **32 Vowels** in Thai language which are divided into

- 18 single vowels
- 6 compound vowels
- 8 consonantlike vowels

Each group comprises of short and long sounds.

All vowels, except ฤ, ฤๅ, ฦๅ, can not stand alone.

❶ สระเดี่ยว (single vowels): 18

เสียงสั้น (short sound)   **เสียงยาว** (long sound)

short			long		
ะ	(อะ)	จะ	า	(อา)	นา
ิ	(อิ)	ติ	ี	(อี)	ดี
ึ	(อึ)	ถึง	ื	(อือ)	มือ

23

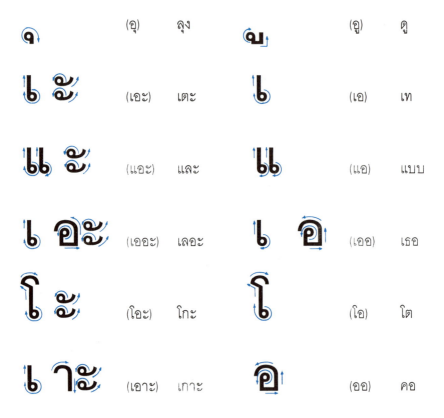

When the vowel ◌ึ does not have a final consonant, อ at the end of the word is needed (such as in the word มือ); it is impossible to write มึ.

อ is a very special alphabet **because อ can be both consonant and vowel.** For example: in the word อา, อ is initial consonant whereas in the word คอ, อ is vowel. Please note that อ as initial is always silent because it is only used to support the vowels which can not stand alone. So in this case, simply read or pronounce the vowel of that word.

แบบฝึกหัดการอ่าน (Reading exercise)

Try to read the following syllables, then check with the cassette. If you can not read them correctly, revise the consonants and vowels once again.

กะ	จะ	ดะ		คา	งาน	สา
กิน	จิม	ดิน		ที	กีด	อีก
อื	ดึง	บืน		มืด	ถือ	คือ
กุด	จุ	สุข		ดู	ขูด	มูม
เอะ	เตะ	เละ		เลว	เดน	เก
แกะ	และ	แทะ		แดด	แก	แสง
เลอะ	เจอะ	เบอะ		เมอ	เธอ	ญอ
โระ	โผะ	โฉะ		โต	โกง	โทน
เกาะ	เจาะ	เคาะ		สอน	ดอย	ตอ

Do not mix up the sounds of vowel อ and โ. อ is pronounced like O in the word pond but โ like in the word go.

แบบฝึกหัดการฟัง (Listening exercise)

Listen to the cassette carefully, then choose the right one from each pair of these following syllables.

จะ	จา	ติ	ตี	บิ	บี	แอะ	เอะ
เกะ	เก	เทอะ	เทาะ	โว	วา	รู	เรอ
ถือ	ถี	เปาะ	ปอ	แคะ	แค	เจอะ	แจะ
แข	เข	ปี	ปู	เลอะ	และ	แท	ทอ

25

แบบฝึกหัดการเขียน (Writing exercise)

Please practise writing vowels several times with any consonant. Be careful with the position of the vowels in words or syllables. A wrong position can lead to a mistake.

❷ สระผสม (compound vowels): 6

เสียงสั้น (short sound)   **เสียงยาว** (long sound)

เ◌ียะ (เอียะ) เกียะ   เ◌ีย (เอีย) เสียง

เ◌ือะ (เอือะ) เกือะ   เ◌ือ (เอือ) เมือง

◌ัวะ   (อัวะ)   กัวะ   ◌ัว   (อัว)   วัว

The 3 short sound compound vowels are seldom needed. They are mainly used to write Chinese names.

❸ สระเกิน (consonantlike vowels): 8 but only 6 are in use.

เสียงสั้น (short sound)   **เสียงยาว** (long sound)

ฤ   (รึ)   ฤดู   ฤๅ ฤๅ (รือ) ฤๅชา

◌ำ   (อำ) คำ

ใ◌   (ใอ) ใจ

ไ   (ไอ)   ไว

เ า   (เอา)   เบา

These vowels sound like they already had a consonant (such as ำ sounds like อะ + ม). ฤๅ or ฦๅ are very rarely used. ฦ is almost just seen in the word ฤดู (season). The two are only vowels which can stand alone as a syllable. For example: there are 2 syllables in the word ฤดู because ฤ is already one by itself.

แบบฝึกหัดการฟัง (Listening exercise)

Listen to the cassette carefully, then choose the right one from each pair of these following syllables.

เสีย	เสื่อ	วัว	โว	เกียะ	เกือก	เมีย	เมือ
ตัว	ตำ	ได	ดาย	เขา	เขือ	เปียะ	เปอะ
นำ	เนา	เพื่อง	เพียง	เคาะ	เคอะ	เดา	ดาว
ใจ	ไซ	มัว	เมือย	เดือน	เดีย	ข่ำ	ขาม

แบบฝึกหัดการอ่าน (Reading exercise)

Try to read the following meaningful words. Check with the cassette. You can find their meanings in the vocabulary list at the end of the lesson.

ตัวดำ	สีทอง	ลูกชาย	คำพูด
แนะนำ	จิตใจ	ภูเขา	เมืองไทย
สาวงาม	สะอาด	แสงแดด	เสียดาย
สายไฟ	เดือนแรม	ชาวเกาะ	รอคอย
ทำนาย	จืดจาง	ยุโรป	เอเซีย
นิยาย	อาหาร	เวลา	การเรียน

แบบฝึกหัดการเขียน (Writing exercise)

Please practise writing vowels several times with any consonant. Be careful with the position of the vowels in words or syllables. A wrong position can lead to a mistake.

บทสนทนา (Dialogue)

ซูซาน	ขอโทษค่ะ คุณชื่ออะไรคะ	Excuse me, please. What is your name?
สุภา	สุภา สุดใจค่ะ คุณล่ะคะ	Supa Sudjai, and you?
ซูซาน	ซูซาน วูดค่ะ มาจากแคนาดา คุณล่ะคะ	Susan Wood. (I) am from Canada, and you?
สุภา	เมืองไทยค่ะ	Thailand.

Remark:

❶ To introduce oneself, it is alright to say both first and last names but in a conversation, the Thai usually use only their first name.

❷ ค่ะ or คะ is particle without meaning (only used by women) but it helps making a sentence more polite and beautiful. ค่ะ is used in an affirmative sentence or when you say "yes". คะ is used in an interrogative sentence or together with the particle นะ in an affirmative sentence.

❸ คุณ is here a pronoun which means "you". Thai language has many words for "you" but คุณ is very polite and can be used in almost all occasions.

❹ When the meaning is clear, a pronoun or noun, no matter as subject or object, can be left out (such as in the sentence มาจากแคนาดา (came from Canada).

Vocabulary:

น.	สระ	-	vowel
ค.,ว.	สั้น	-	short
ค.,ว.	ยาว	-	long
ก.	จะ	-	will, shall
น.	นา	-	field
ก.	ติ	-	blame, criticize
ค.,ว.	ดี	-	good, well
ก.,บ.	ถึง	-	reach, until
น.	มือ	-	hand
น.	ลุง	-	uncle (elder brother of mother or father)
ก.	ดู	-	look
ก.	เตะ	-	kick
ก.	เท	-	pour
บ.,สัน.	และ	-	and, as well as
น.	แบบ	-	model
ค.,ว.	เลอะ	-	very dirty
ส.	เธอ	-	you (not used with older people or those with higher status)
ก.,ค.,ว.	โต	-	grow up, big
น.,ก.	เกาะ	-	island, hold, catch
น.	คอ	-	neck, throat
ก.	อ่าน	-	read
น.	งาน	-	work, job, festival, celebration
ก.	กิน	-	eat
น.	ดิน	-	soil
ว.	อีก	-	again
ก.	ดึง	-	pull

ค.	มืด	-	dark
ก.	ถือ	-	carry, hold, regard
ก.	คือ	-	v. to be
ค.	สุข	-	happy
ค.	เละ	-	very soft, mushy
ค.,ว.	เลว	-	bad
น.,ก.	แกะ	-	sheep, carve
น.	แดด	-	sunlight
ส.	แก	-	you (impolite), he or she (coll.)
น.	แสง	-	light
ก.	โกง	-	cheat
ค.	โทน	-	single
ก.	เจาะ	-	make a hole
ก.	เคาะ	-	knock
ก.	สอน	-	teach
น.	ดอย	-	mountain (northern dialect)
น.	วา	-	a Thai unit of length measurement, about 1.5 meter
น.	รู	-	hole
น.	ปี	-	year
น.	ปู	-	crab
ก.	ทอ	-	weave
ก.,ค.	ผสม	-	mix, compound
น.	เมือง	-	town
น.	วัว	-	cow, ox
ค.	เกิน	-	exceeding, beyond, over
น.	ฤดู	-	season
น.	คำ	-	word
น.	ใจ, จิตใจ	-	mind, heart

ค.,ว.	ไว	-	quick, swift
ค.,ว.	เบา	-	light, not heavy
ค.,ก.	เสีย	-	out of order, decay, lose
น.	เสือ	-	tiger
น.	เมีย	-	wife (coll., not very polite)
น.	ตัว	-	body
ส.	เขา	-	he, she, they
ก.	นำ	-	lead
ว.	เพียง	-	only, just
ก.	เดา	-	guess
น.	ดาว	-	star
ว.	มัว	-	cloudy, dull, blurred, dim
น.	เดือน	-	month, moon
ค.	ดำ	-	black
น.	สีทอง	-	gold colour
น.	ลูกชาย	-	son
น.	คำพูด	-	spoken words
ก.	แนะนำ	-	introduce, advise, recommend
น.	ภูเขา	-	mountain
น.	เมืองไทย	-	Thailand (coll.)
น.	สาว	-	young woman
ค.,ว.	งาม	-	graceful, very beautiful
ค.,ว.	สะอาด	-	clean
ก.,ว.	เสียดาย	-	regretted
น.	สายไฟ	-	cable
น.	เดือนแรม	-	dark moon
น.	ชาวเกาะ	-	islander
ก.	รอคอย	-	wait
ก.	ทำนาย	-	predict, anticipate

ก.	จืดจาง	-	(Love or relation which) dies down with the time or distance
น.	ยุโรป	-	Europe
น.	เอเซีย	-	Asia
น.	นิยาย	-	novel, tale
น.	อาหาร	-	food
น.	เวลา	-	time
ก.	เรียน	-	learn
	ขอโทษ	-	excuse me
ส.	คุณ	-	you
น.,ก.	ชื่อ	-	name, to be called
ส.	อะไร	-	what
ก.	มา	-	come
บ.	จาก	-	from

☑ **Listening exercise** - single vowels

จา	ติ	บี	เอะ	เก	เทาะ	วา	เรอ
ถี	ปอ	แค	เจอะ	เข	ปู	และ	ทอ

☑ **Listening exercise** - compound and consonant like vowels

เสือ	วัว	เกือก	เมีย	ตัว	ได	เขา	เปียะ
นำ	เพียง	เคาะ	เดา	ใจ	เมือย	เดีย	ขำ

Lesson III

วรรณยุกต์ Tones

❶ Thai is a tonal language. Each syllable has always a definite tone. The syllables or words with the same consonants and vowels but different tones are regarded as different syllables or words with different meanings. So although the Thai can probably understand what you mean from the context crew, it is much better to try to pronounce the right tone as clearly as possible. (Please listen carefully to the cassette and try to imitate what you hear). It is advisory that when you are not sure if you can pronounce the right tone or not, you should try to say what you want in a short sentence or phrase, not in one single word. As explained before, a context crew can help your conversation partner to understand you better.

❷ There are in Thai 4 tone marks but 5 tone sounds because the middle tone sound and the basic tones of consonants have no tone mark. Another thing to keep in mind is that not all consonants can have 5 tone sounds. There are certainly rules for this point which you will learn in one of the following lessons.

รูปวรรณยุกต์ (tone marks)   เสียงวรรณยุกต์ (tone sounds)

---   เสียงสามัญ (middle)

่   (ไม้เอก)   เสียงเอก (low)

้	(ไม้โท)	เสียงโท (falling)
๊	(ไม้ตรี)	เสียงตรี (high)
+	(ไม้จัตวา)	เสียงจัตวา (rising)

For Example:

กา   ก่า   ก้า   ก๊า   ก๋า
ดี   ดี่   ดี้   ดี๊   ดี๋

🎧 แบบฝึกหัดการฟัง (Listening exercise)

Listen to the cassette carefully, then choose the right one from each pair of these following syllables.

กา   ก่า   ดู่   ดู๋   ป่า   ป๋า   ตี่   ตี๋
เบ๊   เบ๋   โอ่   โอ๋   จาย   จ่าย   บ้อ   บ๊อ
แก   แก๋   ตู้   ตู๋   ปิ่น   ปิ้น   ใอ   ใอ่

🎧 แบบฝึกหัดการอ่าน (Reading exercise)

Try to read the following words, pay attention also to the tones, and check with the cassette if it is correct or not.

ไก่   ดาว   อุ้ม   จิ๋ว   ตาย   ป้อมแป้ม
ป้อม   เก่า   เดือน   อุ๊ย   จาน   เดี๋ยว
เจ๊า   ป่า   แก้ม   ตุ้ม   บ่อ   บ๊ายบาย
แก่   จ๋า   โอ้   ใจ   บ้าบอ   จุ๋มจิ๋ม

แบบฝึกหัดการเขียน (Writing exercise)

Write a syllable with the tone marks several times. Be careful with their positions.

ดา   ด่า   ด้า   ด๊า   ด๋า

Vocabulary:

น.	วรรณยุกต์	-	tone
น.	รูป	-	form, mark, picture
น.	ไม้	-	wood, sigh, mark
ค.	สามัญ	-	middle, simple, common
น.	ไม้เอก	-	low tone mark
น.	ไม้โท	-	falling tone mark
น.	ไม้ตรี	-	high tone mark
น.	ไม้จัตวา	-	rising tone mark
น.	กา	-	kettle, crow
น.	ป่า	-	forest
ก.	จ่าย	-	pay
ค.,บ	แก่	-	old (not young), to
น.	ตู้	-	cupboard
น.	ไก่	-	chicken
ก.	อุ้ม	-	carry with arms around
ค.	จิ๋ว	-	tiny
ก.	ตาย	-	die
ค.	เก่า	-	old (not new, not fresh)
น.	จาน	-	dish
ว.	เดี๋ยว	-	a moment
น.	แก้ม	-	cheek

น.	บ่อ	-	well
	บ๊าย บาย	-	bye bye
	จ๋า	-	the answer "yes" when being called (coll.)
ค.,ว.	บ้า(บอ)	-	mad, crazy
ค.,ว.	จุ๋มจิ๋ม	-	small and lovely

☑ Listening exercise

| กา | ดู้ | ป้า | ตี่ | เบ๊ | โอ้ | จาย | บ๊อ |
| แก่ | ตู้ | ปิ่น | ใอ | | | | |

Lesson IV

History and main characteristics of Thai language

History:

So far no one can say for sure what the origin of Thai language was; no matter from the language structure or from the historical background. We have known only that King Ramkamhaeng of Sukothai created Thai alphabets in the year 1283, using as its basis the Mon and Khmer scripts which were derived from a south Indian script. Thai alphabets were later several times modified. The current script dates back until the reign of King Rama I (1782 - 1809).

Main characteristics of Thai language:

1. Different from English, words in Thai can be **independently** put in a sentence **without** changing the form due to the various sentence's conditions, such as number, tense, gender, etc. For example:

He *eats* rice.	เขา**กิน**ข้าว
We *eat* rice.	เรา**กิน**ข้าว
This month the weather <u>is</u> *good*.	เดือนนี้อากาศดี
Last month the weather <u>was</u> *good*.	เดือนก่อนอากาศดี

2. As there is no change of the word form, the positions of words in a sentence are extremely important. Wrong positions can cause wrong functions and meanings. Actually a Thai sentence has the same basic structure like in English:

SUBJECT   VERB   OBJECT

But an adverb can not be put between the subject and verb or between the verb and object. The position of the adverb of time or place is normally at the beginning or at the end of the sentence whereas the adverb of manner can only be at the end. For example:

With adverb of time:

เขาดื่มกาแฟ*ตอนเช้า*   He drinks coffee *in the morning*.
*ตอนเช้า*เขาดื่มกาแฟ   or: *In the morning* he drinks coffee.

With adverb of place:

เขาเรียนภาษาไทย*ที่ลอนดอน*   He learns Thai *in London*.
*ที่ลอนดอน*เขาเรียนภาษาไทย   or: *In London* he learns Thai.

With adverb of manner:

เขาว่ายน้ำ*บ่อยมาก*   He swims *very often*.

3. The position of an adjective or adverb is almost always behind its main word. For example:

    beautiful **woman**   สาวงาม
    white **cat**   แมวขาว

very **hot**	ร้อน**มาก**
already **eaten**	**กิน**แล้ว

There are however some rare exceptions which are usually spoken idioms of the meaning "very" or "always". They are: ช่าง ..จอม ..สุด ..ยอด ..แสน .. These adverbs stand in front of their verbs or adjectives.

ช่างคุย	**very** talkative
จอมยุ่ง	**always** making problems
ยอดดื้อ	**very** stubborn
แสนดี	**very** good
สุดเท่	**very** smart

4. An adjective in a sentence which follows verb "to be" is regarded in Thai as a verb. For example:

เขาดี	He **is** good.
บ้านนี้เก่า	This house **is** old.

5. Thai language has no article.

6. Like English, Thai has 2 genders: male and female for human beings and animals.

There are some nouns which we can know from the common sense at once which gender they have, such as พ่อ (father), แม่ (mother), etc.

For others, when needed, a gender can be easily indicated by simply adding an adjective right behind or in front of the main word. Some of the adjectives are:

for human beings:

- ❶ male: ชาย (พี่ชาย elder brother), ผู้ชาย (นายผู้ชาย master), บ่าว (เจ้าบ่าว groom), ...
- ❷ female: สาว (ลูกสาว daughter), สะใภ้ (น้องสะใภ้ sister in law), ...

for animals:

- ❶ male: ตัวผู้ (วัวตัวผู้ ox), พ่อ (พ่อไก่ cock),...
- ❷ female: ตัวเมีย (วัวตัวเมีย cow), แม่ (แม่ไก่ hen), ...

The exception is for elephants (ช้าง) as the male elephant is called ช้างพลาย and the female one ช้างพัง.

Please note that the gender of a noun does not really have effect to other Thai grammar points. For example:

Paul's uncle is called Dam.   ลุงของพอลชื่อดำ

His uncle is called Dam.   ลุงของเขาชื่อดำ

Jane's uncle is called Tim.   ลุงของเจนชื่อทิม

Her uncle is called Tim.   ลุงของเขาชื่อทิม

7. Tense is not a serious point in Thai grammar. It does not cause the change of the word form or the structure of the sentence. The Thai make the tense of their sentences clear by simply using an adverb of time, such as

Last year he <u>learnt</u> Thai.   ปีก่อน เขา<u>เรียน</u>ภาษาไทย

At present he <u>learns</u> Chinese.   ตอนนี้ เขา<u>เรียน</u>ภาษาจีน

Moreover there are a few interesting helping verbs and adverbs which can be used to make the tense clearer, such as

❶ กำลัง... indicates present (or past) continuous tense, e.g.

เขา**กำลัง**ดื่มน้ำ   He **is** drinking water.

Remark: กำลัง is pronounced GAMLANG with the middle tone.

❷ กำลัง...อยู่, ...อยู่ indicates present perfect continuous tense, e.g.

เขา**กำลัง**นอน**อยู่** , เขานอน**อยู่** He **has been** sleeping.

Remark: อยู่ is pronounced YU with the low tone.

❸ ...มา... indicates present perfect tense, e.g.

เขาเรียนภาษาไทย**มา** 2 ปี แล้ว   He **has** already learned Thai **for** 2 years.

❹ จะ... indicates future tense, e.g.

เขา**จะ**บินไปเมืองไทย   He **will** fly to Thailand.

❺ กำลังจะ... indicates a near future, e.g.

เขา**กำลังจะ**นอน   He **is about to** go to bed.

❻ ได้... indicates past tense, e.g.

พี่สาว**ได้**สอบผ่านเมื่อวานนี้   The elder sister pass**ed** the examination yesterday.

❼ แล้ว... can show both past and perfect tenses, e.g.

น้องชายกินข้าว**แล้ว**   The younger brother **ate already**.
เขาไปหัวหิน**แล้ว**   He **has already gone** to Hua Hin.

8. Thai language has classification nouns which mostly stand behind the main words. For example:

    2 eggs   ไข่ 2 **ฟอง** (ฟอง is classification noun for egg)

this blouse เสื้อตัวนี้ (ตัว is classification noun for clothes)

9. One word can have different functions and meanings. This depends on where that word stands in the sentence. For example:

เขาสีไวโอลิน   He **plays** violin.

(สี is here a verb)

น้ำสะอาดไม่มีสี   Clean water has no **colour**.

(สี is here a noun and its function is object.)

10. Thai is a tonal language. The words which have the same initials and finals but different tones are regarded as different words and have different meanings, e.g.

    ขาว   white

    ข่าว   news

    ข้าว   rice

11. Thai has levels of language which depends on age, gender, status, relation between people, etc. In order to use Thai correctly and politely, those conditions must be well considered. For example:

The word เธอ (which also means "you" in English) can not be used with older people or those with a higher status.

12. Thai has very few grammatical marks. There are, for example, no full stop, comma or question mark. If you happen to see them, that just indicates the influence from English and the way the Thai use the marks is also different, such as full stops are only used with abbreviations. For example ร.ร. = โรงเรียน (school), น.ส. = นางสาว (Miss ...). The real Thai grammatical marks that can be often used are

❶ ฯ (ไปยาลน้อย) is used to show that there are still **some more** words which are not written down, e.g. กรุงเทพฯ (Bangkok). ฯ behind กรุงเทพ tells us that the full name of Thailand's capital is about 3 lines long!!!

❷ ฯลฯ (ไปยาลใหญ่) is used to show that there are **many words** which are not written down such as ดอกไม้ไทยมีมากมายคือ มะลิ จำปา ดอกบัว ฯลฯ (There are many kinds of Thai flowers, such as jasmine, champac, lotus, etc.)

Remark: ใหญ่ is pronounced YAI with the low tone.

❸ ๆ (ไม้ยมก - read MAI YAMOOK, all three syllables with high tone) is used to repeat words, phrases or sentences, such as ตอนค่ำๆ (in the evening) is read ตอนค่ำค่ำ. ๆ can be used only when the repeating word has exactly the same spelling, pronunciation and meaning. For example: in the sentence ตาตาบอด (Grandpa is blind), ๆ can not be used because the first ตา means **Grandpa** whereas the second ตา means **eye**.

There are 4 reasons to put ๆ after a word:

① To make that noun or pronoun to be plural, such as เพื่อน means "friend" but เพื่อนๆ means "friends".

② To decrease the accuracy of the meaning, e.g. สีขาว means "white" but สีขาวๆ means "beige or very light colour".

③ To make a kind of spoken idiom, such as ตอนค่ำๆ has the same meaning as ตอนค่ำ but the Thai like to repeat the last word.

④ To make a spoken imperative sentence, such as เขียนดีๆ means "Write it nicely!"

13. In general there is no gap between words in a sentence like in English except when it is needed to make the meaning clear. Unfortunately there is no exact rule to say when you need it. To put a gap at the right place depends more on the feeling one can have for a language which probably happens after getting to know it well enough for a while. For example:

อาหารที่เขาชอบมีไก่ย่าง ข้าวผัด และแกงจืด
The food he likes is grilled chicken, fried rice and clear soup.

Vocabulary:

น.	ข้าว	-	rice
ส.	เรา	-	we, us
ค.	นี้, นั้น	-	this, that
น.	อากาศ	-	weather
ค.	ก่อน	-	last ...
ก.	ดื่ม	-	drink
น.	กาแฟ	-	coffee
น.	ตอนเช้า	-	in the morning
น.	ภาษาไทย	-	Thai language
บ., ส., สัน.	ที่	-	at, in, which
ก.	ว่ายน้ำ	-	swim
ว.	บ่อย	-	often
ค., ว.	มาก(มาย)	-	very, much
น.	แมว	-	cat
น.	(สี) ขาว	-	white
ค., ว.	ร้อน	-	hot

ว.	แล้ว	-	already
ก.	คุย	-	talk
ค.,ว.	ยุ่ง	-	busy, confused, problem making
ค.,ว.	ดื้อ	-	stubborn
ค.,ว.	เท่	-	smart, elegant (coll.)
น.	บ้าน	-	house
น.	พ่อ	-	father
น.	แม่	-	mother
น.,ค.	(ผู้)ชาย	-	man, male
น.	พี่ชาย	-	elder brother
น.	นายผู้ชาย	-	master
น.	บ่าว	-	servant (old language)
น.	เจ้าบ่าว	-	groom
น.	ลูกสาว	-	daughter
น.	....สะใภ้	-	... in law (only female)
น.	น้องสะใภ้	-	sister in law
น.,ค.	ตัวผู้	-	male (animal)
น.,ค.	ตัวเมีย	-	female (animal)
น.	ช้าง	-	elephant
น.,บ.	ของ	-	thing, of
ว.	ตอนนี้	-	at the present
น.	ภาษาจีน	-	Chinese
น.,ว.	กำลัง	-	power, energy, ...ing
น.	น้ำ	-	water
ก.,ว.	อยู่,.......อยู่	-	verb to be, have been ...ing
ก.	นอน	-	sleep
ก.	บิน	-	fly
ก.,บ.	ไป	-	go, to
น.	พี่สาว	-	elder sister

ก.	สอบผ่าน	-	pass an examination
น.	(เมื่อ)วานนี้	-	yesterday
น.	น้องชาย	-	younger brother
น.	ไข่	-	egg
น.	เสื้อ	-	blouse, shirt
น.,ก.	สี	-	colour, play (violin)
ว.	ไม่	-	not
ก.	มี	-	have
น.	ข่าว	-	news
น.	โรงเรียน	-	school
น.	นางสาว	-	Miss
ค.,ว.	น้อย	-	small, little
ค.	ใหญ่	-	big
น.	ดอกไม้	-	flower
น.	มะลิ	-	jasmine
น.	จำปา	-	champac
น.	ดอกบัว	-	lotus
ว.	ตอนค่ำๆ	-	in the evening
น.	ตา	-	grandpa, eye
ก.,ค.	ตาบอด	-	blind
น.	เพื่อน	-	friend
ก.	ชอบ	-	like
ก.	ย่าง	-	grill
ก.	ผัด	-	fry
น.	แกงจืด	-	clear soup

Lesson V

Special rules for vowels

Vowels which sounds are different from the forms and vowels with no form

	form ≠ sound	without form
1 -ะ	1. when -ะ has a final: -ะ → -ั (ไม้หันอากาศ) รัก (ระ + ก) นัด (นะ + ด) ฟัง (ฟะ + ง) ทัน (ทะ + น) 2. รร (ร. หัน) is read like -ะ with a final: วรรณ (วะ + ณ) ธรรม (ธะ + ม) But when there is no final, ร หัน is read like ะ + น. หรรษา (หะ + น + ษา) รังสรรค์ (รัง + สะ + น) Remark: -์ in the word รังสรรค์ is called ไม้ทัณฑฆาต. The consonant with -์ which is called การันต์ can not	1. Leading syllable: A leading syllable looks like a consonant standing alone at the beginning of a word but it must be read like a consonant with half sound of vowel -ะ: ขยัน (ขะ + ยัน) สบาย (สะ + บาย) 2. คำสมาส (Pali and Sanskrit compound words) Owing to Buddhism and Hinduism, Thai language has many vocabularies which derived from Pali and Sanskrit. When more than one of those words are put together (compound words) we have to read them as if there were -ะ.

	be pronounced and is not regarded as a final either.	พิพิธภัณฑ์ (พิ + พิธ + ธะ + ภัณฑ์) รัฐบาล (รัฐ + ฐะ + บาล)
		3. **For authentic Thai words,** when there is no -ะ between two syllables, we usually read them without -ะ, e.g. ดินสอ (ดิน + สอ) But there are also a few exceptions that we have to add half sound of -ะ between syllables, e.g. สัพยอก (สัพ + พะ + ยอก) Exercise: lesson V.I
2 เ-ะ	1. เ-ะ with a final but without a tone mark: เ-ะ → เ ็ (็ is called ไม้ไต่คู้) เพ็ญ (เพะ + ญ)　เต็ม (เตะ + ม) เป็น (เปะ + น)　เห็น (เหะ + น) 2. เ-ะ with a final and a tone mark: เ-ะ → เ เซ่น (เซะ + น)　เก่ง (เกะ + ง) เต้น (เตะ + น)　เล่น (เละ + น) Exercise: lesson V.II	

3 แ-ะ	1. แ-ะ with a final but without a tone mark: แ-ะ ➔ แ ็- แข็ง (แขะ + ง) แท็กซี่ (แทะ + ก + ซี่) 2. แ-ะ with a final and a tone mark: แ-ะ ➔ แ แข่ง (แข่ะ + ง) แต่ง (แต่ะ + ง) แบ่ง (แบ่ะ + ง) แก่ง (แก่ะ + ง) Exercise: lesson V.III
4 เ-อ	1. เ-อ with a final (except ย): เ-อ ➔ เ ิ- เดิน (เดอ + น) เกิด (เกอ + ด) เปิ่น (เปอ + น) เชิญ (เชอ + ญ) 2. เ-อ + ย ➔ เ-ย เคย (เคอ + ย) เต้ย (เต้อ + ย) เซย (เซอ + ย) เนย (เนอ + ย) Exercise: lesson V.IV

5 โ-ะ		1. โ-ะ with a final: มด (โมะ + ด) จด (โจะ + ด) คน (โคะ + น) ผม (โผะ + ม) Exercise: lesson V.V
6 เ-าะ	1. เ-าะ with a final: เ-าะ ➔ ˈ-อ or ˈˈ-อ ก็อด (เกาะ + ด) พล็อต (เพลาะ + ต) ซ็อก (เซาะ + ก) ก็อก (เกาะ + ก) Remark: Most are English words. 2. ก็ is pronounced like เก้าะ.	
7 -อ		1. A syllable with ร as final: -อ disappears and ร is pronounced as น. ละคร (ละ + คอ + ร) พร (พอ + ร) จราจร (จะ + รา + จอ + ร)

		2. When บ stands alone as the first syllable of the word, it is read like บอ: บริการ (บอ + ริ + การ) บริหาร (บอ + ริ + หาร) บริสุทธิ์ (บอ + ริ + สุทธิ์) 3. When จ ท ธ น ม ว ส ษ ห อ is the initial of a syllable and followed by ร, the initial is read as if it had vowel -อ: มรดก (มอ + ระ + ดก) มรกต (มอ + ระ + กต) ทรชน (ทอ + ระ + ชน) Exercise: lesson V.VI
8 -ัว	1. -ัว with a final ̆ disappears: -ัว ➜ -ว- ขวด (ขัว + ด) ปวด (ปัว + ด) ป่วย (ปั่ว + ย) สวย (สัว + ย) Exercise: lesson V.VI	

Vocabulary:

ก.	รัก	-	love
น.	นัด	-	date, appointment
ว.	ทัน	-	on time, punctual
ก.,ค.,ว.	ขยัน	-	industrious
ค.,ว.	สบาย	-	comfortable
น.	พิพิธภัณฑ์	-	museum
น.	รัฐบาล	-	government
น.	ดินสอ	-	pencil
ก.	สัพยอก	-	to kid, pull one's leg
ค.	เต็ม	-	full
ก.	เป็น	-	verb to be
ก.	เห็น	-	see
	เช่น	-	for example, such as
ค.,ว.	เก่ง	-	good in doing sth.
ก.	เต้น	-	dance
ก.	เล่น	-	play
ค.	แข็ง	-	hard
น.	แท็กซี่	-	taxi
ก.	แข่ง	-	compete
ก.	แต่ง	-	decorate
ก.	แบ่ง	-	separate
ก.	เดิน	-	walk
ก.	เกิด	-	happen, to be born
ก.,ว.	เปิ่น	-	old-fashioned, embarrassed
ก.	เชิญ	-	invite
ก.	เคย	-	used to
ค.	เชย	-	old-fashioned

น.	เนย	-	butter
น.	มด	-	ant
ก.	จด	-	note
น.	คน	-	human being
ส.,น.	ผม	-	- I (male only) - hair
น.	ละคร	-	play (theatre)
น.	พร	-	wish
น.	จราจร	-	traffic
ก.	บริการ	-	serve
ก.	บริหาร	-	administrate
ค.	บริสุทธิ์	-	pure, innocent
น.	มรดก	-	heritage
น.	มรกต	-	emerald
น.	ทรชน	-	bad people
น.	ขวด	-	bottle
ก.	ปวด	-	have pain
ก.,ค.	ป่วย	-	ill
ค.,ว.	สวย	-	beautiful

Lesson V.I

Exercises for vowel -ะ

🎧 แบบฝึกหัดการฟัง

Listen to the cassette carefully, then choose the right word from each pair of words below.

การ	กัน	ทัน	ทาน	มัน	มาร	ฟัง	ฟาง
จาน	จัน	ขาบ	ขับ	กาด	กัด	บัด	บาท
วัน	วาน	ชาน	ชัน	บัง	บาง	หัด	หาด

Remark: Please note that ̃ must be shortly pronounced because it is in fact vowel -ะ.

🎧 แบบฝึกหัดการอ่าน

Try to read the following words, then check with the cassette if it is right or not.

สตางค์	ขโมย	สบาย	สะพาน
กะทิ	ภรรยา	บังคับ	สวัสดี
การพนัน	พิพิธภัณฑ์	ถนัด	นิสัย
สัญญา	ธรรมชาติ	วัฒนธรรม	เยอรมัน

Remark: Between สวัส and ดี in the word สวัสดี, as well as between สัญ and ญา in the word สัญญา, we read without -ะ although สวัสดี is Sanskrit

and สัญญา is Pali because they are one single word, not compound word.
- In the word ธรรมชาติ, ชาติ is usually pronounced ชาต as if there were no ิ.
- The word ภรรยา can be read both PANYA and PANRAYA.

⊛ แบบฝึกหัดการพูด

❶ This exercise is aimed to help you to practise pronunciation and get used to some easy sentence structures. Try to figure out the meaning yourself with the help of the vocabulary list.

ใจดี	A	เขาใจดีนะคะ	B	ครับ ใจดีมาก
เก่ง	A	เขาเก่งนะคะ	B	ครับ เก่งที่สุด
ดุ	A	เขาดุนะคะ	B	ครับ ดุจริงๆ
สูง	A	เขาสูงนะคะ	B	ครับ ค่อนข้างสูง

Now please try to make sentences yourself from the structures you have learned.

ภาษาไทย.....................ง่าย   ยาก   สนุก   น่าเบื่อ

Remark: In the word จริงๆ, จร is pronounced like จ and ๆ is repeating mark.

❷ Here is another exercise to practise pronunciation. Mr. **A** says that he likes something, then he asks Miss **B** "What about you?". There are surely both negative and positive answers.

กิน	อาหารไทย	A	เขาชอบกินอาหารไทย	แล้วคุณล่ะครับ
ดื่ม	เบียร์	A	เขาชอบดื่มเบียร์	แล้วคุณล่ะครับ
นอนดึก		A	เขาชอบนอนดึก	แล้วคุณล่ะครับ
ทำงาน		A	เขาชอบทำงาน	แล้วคุณล่ะครับ

คำตอบ(Answer)　B　ดิฉันก็ชอบค่ะ

　　　　　　　　　B　ดิฉันไม่ชอบค่ะ

Remark: ก็ is pronounced like เก้าะ and ็ is called ไม้ไต่คู้. ก็ is used in many situations. Here ก็ shows consequences and means "also".

❸ In this exercise, someone tells you what she is doing, then she asks you "What about you?" or "What are you doing?"

ทำอาหาร	ดิฉัน**กำลัง**ทำอาหารค่ะ	คุณกำลังทำอะไรคะ
ทำการบ้าน	ดิฉัน**กำลัง**ทำการบ้านค่ะ	แล้วคุณล่ะคะ
ทำงานบ้าน	ดิฉัน**กำลัง**ทำงานบ้านค่ะ	คุณกำลังทำอะไรคะ
อาบน้ำ	ดิฉัน**กำลัง**อาบน้ำค่ะ	แล้วคุณล่ะคะ
รีดผ้า	ดิฉัน**กำลัง**รีดผ้าค่ะ	คุณกำลังทำอะไรคะ

❹ This exercise tells you how the Thai talk about the future. They simply put จะ (will) in front of the main verb. Please note that จะ is not really needed if it is clear from the context clue that you are talking about the future.

ไปเที่ยว	น้องจะไปนอน	แต่พี่จะไปเที่ยว
ไปโรงเรียน	น้องจะไปเที่ยว	แต่พี่จะไปโรงเรียน
ดูโทรทัศน์	น้องจะไปโรงเรียน	แต่พี่จะดูโทรทัศน์
ฟังวิทยุ	น้องจะดูโทรทัศน์	แต่พี่จะฟังวิทยุ

บทสนทนา (Dialogue)

A สวัสดีครับ คุณกัญญา — Hello Ms. Ganya.

B สวัสดีค่ะ คุณพนัส สบายดีหรือคะ — Hello Mr. Panat. How are you?

A ครับ สบายดี คุณล่ะครับ — I am fine, and you?

B สบายดีค่ะ ขอบคุณค่ะ — So am I, thank you.

Remark:

- สวัสดี can be used as greeting or as good bye at any time of the day.

- The Thai do not shake hands. While saying สวัสดี, the younger or those with a lower status greet the elder or those with a higher status with "WAI". It is a Thai way of showing respectation by putting the two hands together in front of the breast while bowing the head a little bit down.

- คุณ in front of a first name does not have any meaning but it is a polite way to call someone, especially when that person is not very close to you.

- In the word หรือ, ห is not pronounced but ร takes the rising tone from ห.

- Please keep in mind that กัญญา and พนัส are first names.

แบบฝึกหัดการเขียน

Please write several times วันศุกร์ (⁹), มากๆ (ๆ) and ก็ (๘)

Vocabulary:

น.,ก.	ทาน	-	giving, eat (coll.)
ส.	มัน	-	it
น.	มาร	-	devil
น.	ฟาง	-	straw
ก.	ขับ	-	drive
ก.	กัด	-	bite
น.	บาท	-	Baht (฿)
น.	วัน	-	day
น.	ชาน	-	outskirt
ค.	ชัน	-	steep
ค.	บาง	-	thin
ก.	หัด	-	practise
น.	หาด	-	beach
น.	สตางค์	-	money (coll.)
น.,ก.	ขโมย	-	thief, steal
น.	สะพาน	-	bridge
น.	กะทิ,กระทิ	-	coconut milk
น.	ภรรยา	-	wife
ก.	บังคับ	-	force
	สวัสดี	-	Hello, ... (greeting), goodbye
น.	การพนัน	-	gambling
ค.,ว.	ถนัด	-	skilful
น.	นิสัย	-	habit

น.,ก.	สัญญา	-	contract, promise, to promise
น.	ธรรมชาติ	-	nature
น.	วัฒนธรรม	-	culture
น.,ค.	เยอรมัน	-	German
ก.,ค.	ใจดี	-	kind
ก.,ค.	ดุ	-	strict, fierce
ว.	ที่สุด	-	the ...est (superlative degree)
ว.	จริง,จริงๆ	-	really (coll.)
ว.	ค่อนข้าง	-	rather
ค.,ว.	ง่าย	-	easy
ค.,ว.	ยาก	-	difficult
ค.,ว.	สนุก	-	funny, enjoyable
ค.	น่าเบื่อ	-	boring
น.,ว.	ไทย	-	Thai
น.	เบียร์	-	beer
ค.,ว.	ดึก	-	late at night
ก.	ทำ	-	do, make
ก.	ทำงาน	-	work
น.	การบ้าน	-	homework
น.	งานบ้าน	-	household job
ก.	อาบน้ำ	-	have shower, bath
ก.	รีดผ้า	-	to iron
ก.	ไปเที่ยว	-	to go out for pleasure, to have holidays
น.	น้อง	-	younger brother or sister
สัน.	แต่	-	but
น.	พี่	-	elder brother or sister
น.	โทรทัศน์	-	television
น.	วิทยุ	-	radio

| ขอบคุณ | - thank you |

☑ Listening exercise

| กัน | ทัน | มาร | ฟัง | จาน | ขับ | กัด | บาท |
| วัน | ชาน | บาง | หัด | | | | |

Lesson V.II

Exercises for vowel เ-ะ

แบบฝึกหัดการฟัง

Listen to the cassette carefully, then choose the right word from each pair of words below.

เวร	เว้น	เป๋	เป้ง	เข็ญ	เขน	เล็ง	เลน
เคม	เค็ม	เด่น	เด่	เจน	เจ็น	เกะ	เก็ด
เต้น	เตน	เห็น	เหน	เอะ	เอ็น	เบน	เบ็น

แบบฝึกหัดการอ่าน

Try to read the following words, then check with the cassette if it is right or not.

ใจเย็น	เป็นไข้	พูดเท็จ	เจ็บใจ
ตัวเก็ง	เห็นใจ	การเล่น	เว้นวรรค
สำเร็จ	เช่นกัน	ประเทศ	เวรกรรม
เหตุการณ์	สังเกต	เพศชาย	เต็มใจ

Remark: In the word เหตุการณ์ , เหตุ is read as if it were written เหต.

แบบฝึกหัดการพูด

With this exercise you will learn how to ask the names of things politely in Thai, how to say thank you and the answer to it.

โต๊ะ

A ขอโทษครับ นี่ภาษาไทยเรียกว่าอะไรครับ B โต๊ะค่ะ

A ขอบคุณครับ B ไม่เป็นไรค่ะ

เก้าอี้

A ขอโทษครับ นี่ภาษาไทยเรียกว่าอะไรครับ B เก้าอี้ค่ะ

A ขอบคุณครับ B ไม่เป็นไรค่ะ

ดินสอ

A ขอโทษครับ นี่ภาษาไทยเรียกว่าอะไรครับ B ดินสอค่ะ

A ขอบคุณครับ B ไม่เป็นไรค่ะ

ปากกา

A ขอโทษครับ นี่ภาษาไทยเรียกว่าอะไรครับ B ปากกาค่ะ

A ขอบคุณครับ B ยินดีค่ะ

กระดาษ

A ขอโทษครับ นี่ภาษาไทยเรียกว่าอะไรครับ B กระดาษค่ะ

A ขอบคุณครับ B ยินดีค่ะ

แว่นตา

A ขอโทษครับ นี่ภาษาไทยเรียกว่าอะไรครับ B แว่นตาค่ะ

A ขอบคุณครับ B ยินดีค่ะ

Remark: ว่า is here "that". ว่า is needed behind many verbs, such as คิด (think), พูด (say), เล่า (tell), รู้สึก (feel), รู้ (know), etc.

⊕ บทสนทนา (Dialogue)

เดือนเพ็ญ	สวัสดีค่ะ คุณวันชาติ	Hello, Mr. Wanshat.
วันชาติ	สวัสดีครับ คุณเดือนเพ็ญ	Hello, Ms. Deuanpen. Ms.
	คุณเดือนเพ็ญครับ	Deuanpen, this is Kannikar,
	นี่กรรณิการ์ น้องสาวของจิตครับ	Jit's younger sister.
เดือนเพ็ญ	สวัสดีค่ะ คุณกรรณิการ์	Hello, Ms. Kannikar. I am
	ยินดีที่ได้รู้จักคุณค่ะ	pleased to get to know you.
กรรณิการ์	เช่นกันค่ะ คุณเดือนเพ็ญ	So am I, Ms. Deuanpen.

⊕ แบบฝึกหัดการอ่าน

The vocabulary list will help you to understand this short but useful reading exercise.

สัปดาห์มีเจ็ดวันได้แก่

วันจันทร์	วันอังคาร	วันพุธ	วันพฤหัสบดี
วันศุกร์	วันเสาร์	และ	วันอาทิตย์

Remark: Be careful. You may here many Thais read สัปดาห์ like สับ + ปะ + ดา That is definitely wrong. สัปดาห์ is an exception of Sanskrit words. It must be read สับ + ดา.

⊕ แบบฝึกหัดการอ่าน

โทนี่เป็นชาวอเมริกัน แต่เขาชอบเมืองไทยมาก
โทนี่อายุสี่สิบเอ็ดปี เขาแต่งงานแล้วกับสาวไทย
โทนี่มีลูกชายชื่อเควินกับมาร์ค

ตั้งแต่วันจันทร์ถึงวันศุกร์ ตอนกลางวันโทนี่ไปทำงาน
แต่ตอนค่ำๆของเกือบทุกวัน เขาเรียนภาษาไทยกับภรรยา
เขารู้ว่าภาษาไทยไม่ยากมากแต่ก็ไม่ง่ายนัก
เขาจึงตั้งใจเรียนและขยันทำการบ้าน

โปรดตอบคำถามต่อไปนี้

Please answer the following questions.

1. โทนี่เป็นชาว**อะไร**

2. เขาอายุ**เท่าไร**

3. เขายังเป็นโสด**หรือ**แต่งงานแล้ว

4. โทนี่มีลูกชาย**หรือ**ลูกสาว

5. เขาเรียนภาษาไทย**เมื่อไร**

6. **ใคร**สอนภาษาไทยโทนี่

7. **ทำไม**เขาเรียนภาษาไทย

Remark: Living together without or before marriage is not yet completely accepted in Thai society. The Thai have a few words for husband and wife but what you really need is สามี for husband and ภรรยา for wife.

Vocabulary:

น.	เวร	-	turn, fate
ก.,บ.	เว้น	-	leave out, except
ก.	เล็ง	-	to aim, to point
น.	เลน	-	mud
ค.	เค็ม	-	salty

ค.,ว.	เด่น	-	outstanding
ค.	ใจเย็น	-	calm
ก.	เป็นไข้	-	have fever
ก.	พูดเท็จ	-	to lie
ก.,ค.	เจ็บ	-	to feel hurt
ก.	เจ็บใจ	-	furious
น.	ตัวเก็ง	-	favourite
ก.	เห็นใจ	-	to understand and share the feeling
ก.	เว้นวรรค	-	gab between words or sentences
ก.	สำเร็จ	-	successful
	เช่นกัน	-	so do I, so am I
น.	ประเทศ	-	country
น.	เวรกรรม	-	bad turn, retribution
น.	เหตุการณ์	-	event
ก.	สังเกต	-	observe
น.	เพศชาย	-	male
ก.,ว.	เต็มใจ	-	willing
ส.	นี่	-	this, here
ก.	เรียก	-	call
	ไม่เป็นไร	-	you are welcome, it does not matter
น.	โต๊ะ	-	table
น.	เก้าอี้	-	chair
น.	ปากกา	-	pen
	ยินดี	-	you are welcome, to be pleased
น.	กระดาษ	-	paper
น.	แว่นตา	-	glasses
ก.	รู้จัก	-	know
น.	สัปดาห์	-	week
น.	เจ็ด	-	7

	ได้แก่	-	as follow
น.	วันจันทร์	-	Monday
น.	วันอังคาร	-	Tuesday
น.	วันพุธ	-	Wednesday
น.	วันพฤหัสบดี	-	Thursday
น.	วันศุกร์	-	Friday
น.	วันเสาร์	-	Saturday
น.	วันอาทิตย์	-	Sunday
น.	ชาวอเมริกัน	-	American
น.	สี่สิบเอ็ด	-	41
ก.	แต่งงาน	-	marry
บ.	กับ	-	with, and
บ.	ตั้งแต่.....ถึง....	-	since … until
น.,ว.	ตอนกลางวัน	-	at daytime
ว.	เกือบ	-	almost
ค.	ทุก	-	every
ก.	รู้	-	know
ว.	นัก	-	very
สัน.	จึง	-	so, thus
ก.,ว.	ตั้งใจ	-	to concentrate in
ว.	โปรด	-	please
ก.	ตอบ	-	answer
น.	คำถาม	-	question
ค.	ต่อไปนี้	-	following
น., ก.	อายุ	-	age
ส.	เท่าไร	-	how much, how many
ว.	ยัง	-	still
ค.	โสด	-	to be single
สัน.	หรือ	-	or

ส.	เมื่อไร	-	when?
ส.	ใคร	-	who?
ส.	ทำไม	-	why?
สัน.	เพราะ(ว่า)	-	because

☑ Listening exercise

เว้น   เป้   เข็ญ   เลน   เคม   เด่   เจน   เก็ด
เต้น   เห็น   เอะ   เบน

☑ Reading exercise

1.ชาวอเมริกัน   2.สี่สิบเอ็ดปี

3.แต่งงานแล้ว   4.ลูกชาย

5.ตอนค่ำๆของเกือบทุกวัน   6.ภรรยาของโทนี่

7.เพราะว่าเขาชอบเมืองไทยมากและเขาแต่งงานกับสาวไทย

Lesson V.III

Exercises for vowel แ-ะ

🎧 แบบฝึกหัดการฟัง

Listen to the cassette carefully, then choose the right word from each pair of words below.

แกะ	แก่ง	แข็ง	แข	แต่ง	แต่	แลก	และ
เบะ	แบะ	เยอะ	แยะ	แระ	แร้ง	แพะ	เพะ
แวด	แวะ	แดด	แด่ง	แช่ง	แช่	แท้	แท็ก

🎧 แบบฝึกหัดการอ่าน

Try to read the following words, then check with the cassette if it is right or not.

ลูกแกะ	แตะต้อง	แนะนำ	แจ่มใส
แจกัน	แพะรับบาป	แข่งขัน	ข้าวแฉะ
แข็งแรง	แต่งงาน	แบ่งปัน	ของแถม
ใจแคบ	มีแวว	แก้วตา	คะแนน

🎧 บทสนทนา (Dialogue)

ดอริส	ขอโทษค่ะ กี่โมงแล้วคะ	Excuse me, please. What time is it?
แสนสุข	เที่ยงครึ่งครับ	Half past twelve.
ดอริส	ดิฉันไม่เข้าใจค่ะ	I don't understand. What does
	เที่ยงครึ่งแปลว่าอะไรคะ	"half past twelve" mean?

แสนสุข	สิบสองนาฬิกา สามสิบนาทีครับ	Twelve o'clock, thirty minutes.
ดอริส	ขอโทษค่ะ ดิฉันฟังไม่ทัน กรุณาพูดช้าๆอีกทีได้ไหมคะ	Sorry, it is too fast for me to understand. Could you please say it slowly once again?
แสนสุข	สิบ สอง นา ฬิ กา สาม สิบ นา ที ครับ	Twelve o'clock, thirty minutes.
ดอริส	ขอบคุณมากค่ะ	Thank you.
แสนสุข	ยินดีครับ	You're welcome.

Remark:

- There are 2 words which the Thai usually use to say "thank you" They are ขอบคุณ and ขอบใจ. ขอบคุณ is very polite and can be almost always used whereas ขอบใจ is used among close friends or by older people or those with higher status when they talk to the younger or those with a lower status.

- The Thai hardly say "thank you" to those who do service jobs such as waiters, taxi drivers,...

- The answers to "thank you" which are often used are ไม่เป็นไร and ยินดี.

แบบฝึกหัดการพูด

This exercise tells you how to express your surprise to your conversation partner about something. Surely he may agree or disagree with your opinions.

แปลกจัง   ทำไมฝรั่งชอบอาบแดด

แปลกจัง	ทำไมชาวไทยชอบยิ้ม
แปลกนะ	ทำไมชาวอังกฤษชอบดูฟุตบอล
แปลกนะ	ทำไมครูชอบให้การบ้าน
แปลกจริง	ทำไมนักเรียนไม่ชอบทำการบ้าน

คำตอบ   นั่นซิ   ดิฉันก็ไม่เข้าใจเหมือนกัน
          ไม่เห็นแปลก   ผมเองก็ชอบเหมือนกัน

Remark: - In the word เหมือนกัน , ห is not pronounced but ม gets the rising tone from ห.
- ผม is read POOM with the rising tone.

แบบฝึกหัดการอ่าน

    น้ำตาลเป็นลูกสาวนักธุรกิจ เขาอายุสิบปี น้ำตาลมีพี่สาวชื่อนุช และมีน้องชายชื่อแตงโม ครอบครัวของเขามีบ้านที่ริมแม่น้ำแม่กลอง ในเมืองราชบุรี

    น้ำตาลไปโรงเรียนตอนเช้าตั้งแต่วันจันทร์ถึงวันศุกร์ ตอนเย็นเขาเรียนพิเศษที่บ้าน ในวันเสาร์ เขามักจะไปว่ายน้ำหรือเรียนเทนนิส

    น้ำตาลไม่ชอบทำการบ้าน เขาจึงเรียนไม่เก่งเหมือนพี่สาว คุณแม่บอกว่า ถ้าเขาตั้งใจเรียน ตอนโรงเรียนปิด คุณพ่อจะพาไปเที่ยวยุโรป

    น้ำตาลหัวเราะ คุณแม่เข้าใจผิดแล้ว น้ำตาลไม่ต้องการไปเมืองนอกเพราะเขาไม่ชอบอาหารฝรั่ง

    น้ำตาลชอบอยู่บ้านเพราะได้วิ่งเล่นกับพี่น้องและเพื่อนๆ ได้ดูโทรทัศน์ และยังได้รับประทานอาหารไทยอร่อยๆที่คุณย่าทำ

Remark: ราชบุรี can be read both ราด - บุ - รี and ราด - ชะ - บุ - รี.

โปรดตอบคำถามต่อไปนี้

1. คุณพ่อของน้ำตาลมีอาชีพอะไร
2. บ้านของเขาอยู่ที่ไหน
3. พี่สาวของน้ำตาลชื่ออะไร
4. แตงโมคือใคร
5. ตั้งแต่วันจันทร์ถึงวันศุกร์ น้ำตาลทำอะไร
6. ในวันเสาร์ เขาทำอะไร
7. ทำไมน้ำตาลเรียนไม่เก่ง
8. ถ้าเขาตั้งใจเรียน คุณพ่อจะพาไปเที่ยวที่ไหน
9. ทำไมน้ำตาลไม่ชอบไปเมืองนอก
10. ใครทำอาหารอร่อย

Several grammatical functions and meanings of ให้.

❶ to give: ครู**ให้**การบ้าน (แก่) นักเรียน   The teacher **gives** students homework.

❷ to let: ให้เขาดู   **Let** him see.

❸ to: แม่บอก**ให้**ลูกนอน   The mother tells the child **to** sleep.

❹ for: พ่อซื้อเสื้อ**ให้**ลูกชาย   The father buys a shirt **for** the son.

❺ ให้ as special idioms:

- (ให้)เช่า to let: เขามีบ้าน(ให้)เช่า He has a house to let.

- The idioms ทำให้ได้, พูดให้ดี, วิ่งให้เร็ว, คิดให้ถูก ...are used mainly in imperative sentences or to show a strong will.

ทำให้ได้:   คุณต้อง**ทำให้ได้**   You must **be able** to do it.

The word **ได้** in the idiom **ทำให้ได้** means "can", but its function in Thai grammar is an adverb. So you can see that the structure of these idioms is:

Verb + ให้ + Adverb

Vocabulary:

ก.	แลก	-	to exchange
ค.,ว.	เยอะ(แยะ)	-	very much (coll.)
น.	แพะ	-	goat
ก.	แวะ	-	drop in
ก.	แช่ง	-	to curse
ก.	แช่	-	to soak
ค.	แท้	-	real
ก.	แตะ(ต้อง)	-	to touch
ค.	แจ่มใส	-	bright
น.	แจกัน	-	vase
น.	แพะรับบาป	-	scapegoat
ก.	แข่งขัน	-	compete
น.	ข้าวแฉะ	-	too wet cooked rice
ค.	แข็งแรง	-	strong
ก.	แบ่งปัน	-	to share
น.	ของแถม	-	supplement

ก.,ค.	ใจแคบ	-	narrow minded
ก.	มีแวว	-	to show
น.	แก้วตา	-	eyeball
น.	คะแนน	-	marks, points
ว.	กี่......	-	how many
น.	เที่ยง	-	midday
ค.	ครึ่ง	-	half
ก.	เข้าใจ	-	understand
ก.	แปล	-	to mean
น.	สิบสอง	-	12
น.	นาฬิกา	-	o'clock, clock, watch
น.	สามสิบ	-	30
น.	นาที	-	minute
ก.	ฟังไม่ทัน	-	too quick to understand
ว.	กรุณา	-	please
ว.	อีกที	-	again
ก.,ว.	ได้	-	get, can
ว.,น.	ไหม	-	a question tag
ค.,ว.	แปลก	-	strange
ว.	จัง	-	very (coll.)
น.,ค.	ฝรั่ง	-	white people (coll.)
ก.	อาบแดด	-	to have sunbath
ก.,น.	ยิ้ม	-	smile
	นะ	-	a particle in spoken language
น.,ค.	อังกฤษ	-	British
น.	ฟุตบอล	-	football
น.	ครู	-	teacher
ก.	ให้	-	give, let
น.	นักเรียน	-	pupil

	นั่นซิ	-	that's it
ว.,ค.	เหมือนกัน	-	also
	ไม่เห็นแปลก	-	(I) do not find it strange
ว.	เอง	-	oneself
น.	นักธุรกิจ	-	businessman
น.	สิบ	-	10
น.	ครอบครัว	-	family
บ.	ริม	-	on, at, at the edge of ...
น.	แม่น้ำ	-	river
น.,ว.	ตอนเย็น	-	late afternoon
ก.	เรียนพิเศษ	-	to have an extra tuition
ว.	มัก(จะ)	-	often
ค.,ว.	เหมือน	-	like
ก.	บอก	-	to tell
สัน.	ถ้า	-	if
ว.	ตอนโรงเรียนปิด	-	during vacation
ก.	พา	-	to take to ...
น.	เมืองนอก	-	abroad
ก.	หัวเราะ	-	laugh
ค.,ว.	ผิด	-	wrong
ก.	ต้องการ	-	want
ก.	วิ่ง	-	run
น.	พี่น้อง	-	brothers and sisters, relatives
น.	(คุณ)ย่า	-	grandma (father's mother)
ค.	อร่อย	-	delicious
น.	อาชีพ	-	occupation
ส.	ที่ไหน	-	where
น.	ลูก	-	child
ก.	ซื้อ	-	buy

ก.	เช่า	- rent
ค.,ว.	เร็ว	- quick, fast
ก.	คิด	- think
ค.,ว.	ถูก	- correct, cheap

☑ Listening exercise

แก่ง   แข   แต่   แลก   เบะ   เยอะ   แร้ง   แพะ
แวด   แดด   แซ่   แท้

☑ Reading exercise

1. นักธุรกิจ
2. ริมแม่น้ำแม่กลอง เมืองราชบุรี
3. นุช
4. น้องชายของน้ำตาล
5. เรียนหนังสือ
6. ว่ายน้ำหรือเรียนเทนนิส
7. เขาไม่ชอบทำการบ้าน
8. ยุโรป
9. เขาไม่ชอบอาหารฝรั่ง
10. คุณย่า

Lesson V.IV

Exercises for vowel เ-อ

🎧 แบบฝึกหัดการฟัง

Listen to the cassette carefully, then choose the right word from each pair of words below.

เธอ	เทิน	เขย	เขิน	เมิน	เมย	เจอะ	เจอ
เซย	เชิญ	เลิก	เลข	เถิด	เถอะ	เอย	เอิน
เผิน	เผย	เคย	เคน	เดิน	เดิง	เฉอ	เฉย

🎧 แบบฝึกหัดการอ่าน

Try to read the following words, then check with the cassette if it is right or not.

วันเกิด	เยอะแยะ	ละเมอ	บัตรเชิญ
เนยแข็ง	เปิดเผย	ลูกเขย	ผิวเผิน
บังเอิญ	ยายเซย	การเดิน	เทิดทูน
เคยชิน	ขัดเขิน	เบิกบาน	เฉยเมย

Remark: In the word บัตรเชิญ, บัตร is read as if it were written บัต.

แบบฝึกหัดการพูด

คุณพูดไทยเก่งจัง   เรียนภาษาไทยมานานแล้วหรือคะ

คำตอบ   ยังไม่ถึงปีเลยครับ
ประมาณครึ่งปีเท่านั้นครับ
เพิ่งจะสี่เดือนเท่านั้นครับ
ราวๆห้าปีแล้วครับ
ตั้งสิบปีแล้วครับ

In this exercise you learn to use some adverb phrases which can reflect your opinions about what you are talking.

Someone admires you that you can speak very good Thai, than she asks how long you have learned the language. The answer ยังไม่ถึง ... เลย (less than, shorter than) shows that you think the time you have learned Thai is not long at all (so you must be really good!!!). ประมาณ ... เท่านั้น (only about) and เพิ่งจะ ... เท่านั้น (just only about) show the same direction of the attitude behind your answer.

But if you think that the time you have learned Thai is pretty long, the word แล้ว (already) in ราวๆ ... แล้ว helps expressing this opinion.

The word ตั้ง ... does not have any real meaning in English but it definitely helps you to express your feeling that you have spent soooo long time in learning this language. We can say easily that:

$$ตั้ง \neq เท่านั้น$$

By the way มา in the question เรียนภาษาไทยมานานแล้วหรือคะ does not mean "to come". มา in this case is an adverb to indicate present perfect tense.

🎧 บทสนทนา (Dialogue)

วันชาติ	คุณเดือนเพ็ญ ขอโทษครับที่ผมมาสาย เมื่อเช้านี้ มีอุบัติเหตุ เกิดขึ้นในซอย ผมผ่านออกมาไม่ได้ เสียเวลาไปตั้งเกือบชั่วโมง	Ms. Deuanpen, I am sorry that I am late. This morning there was an accident in the lane. I could not pass it, I wasted almost one hour.
เดือนเพ็ญ	ไม่เป็นไรค่ะ ดิฉันเข้าใจ	That's all right, I understand.

Remark: อุบัติเหตุ is pronounced อุ + บัด + ติ + เหตุ.

- The best word to excuse oneself is ขอโทษ. The Thai also use this word before asking someone something. In general the answer to ขอโทษ is ไม่เป็นไร but ไม่เป็นไร in this case means "it is all right" or "it doesn't matter".

- The Thai are usually not very punctual. For a private appointment, being late for some minutes is quite normal.

- The Thai do not like confrontation. For a well brought up Thai, showing strong emotion or aggressiveness means bad manners. Hence, the word ไม่เป็นไร is often used in daily life.

🎧 บทสนทนา (Dialogue)

กรรณิการ์	คุณศิริ ดิฉันเพิ่งได้ข่าวว่า คุณพ่อของคุณเสีย	Mr. Siri, I have just known that your father passed away.

	เสียใจด้วยนะคะ	I am sorry (with you).
ศิร	ขอบคุณครับ คุณกรรณิการ์	Thank you, Ms. Kannikar.

Remark: ด้วย is pronounced "DUAY" with the falling tone.

Several grammatical functions and meanings of เสีย.

❶ die: คุณพ่อของคุณเสีย - Your father **passed away**.
เสีย is the polite word for **to die**. We use เสีย in this meaning only with human beings.

❷ out of order: วิทยุเสีย - The radio is **out of order**.

❸ decay/
turn bad: ไข่เสีย - The egg is **decayed**.

❹ waste, lose: เขาเสียเงินมากกับการพนัน - He **wasted** much money with gambling.

❺ special idioms: เสียใจ (to feel sorry), เสียรู้ (to be betrayed), เสียหน้า (to lose one's face), เสียคำพูด (to break a promise), เสียสติ (to be mad), ท้องเสีย (to have diarrhoea), หน้าเสีย (to turn pale),...

Vocabulary:

น.,ค.	เขย	- ...in law (only male)
ค.,ว.	เขิน	- shy
ก.	เมิน	- turn the eyes away
ก.	เจอ	- see, meet (mainly coincidentally)
ก.	เลิก	- give up
น.	เลข	- number
ค.	เผิน, ผิวเผิน	- superficial, shallow

ก.,ค.	เผย, เปิดเผย	-	reveal, open
น.	วันเกิด	-	birthday
ก.	ละเมอ	-	talk in sleeping
น.	บัตรเชิญ	-	invitation card
น.	เนยแข็ง	-	cheese
น.	ลูกเขย	-	son in law
ว.	บังเอิญ	-	coincidentally
ก.	เทิดทูน	-	adore
ก.,ค.	เคยชิน	-	be used to
ค.,ว.	เบิกบาน	-	cheerful
ก.,ค.	เฉยเมย	-	indifferent
ว.	นาน	-	long (time)
ว.	เลย	-	at all
ว.	ประมาณ, ราวๆ	-	about
ว.	เท่านั้น	-	only
ว.	เพิ่ง(จะ)	-	just
น.	สี่	-	4
น.	ห้า	-	5
ว.	สาย	-	late
ว.	เมื่อเช้านี้	-	this morning
ก.	มี....เกิดขึ้น	-	there is, ... take place
น.	อุบัติเหตุ	-	accident
บ.	ใน	-	in
น.	ซอย	-	lane
ก.	ผ่านออกมา	-	pass (out)
ก.	เสียเวลา	-	waste time
ส.	ดิฉัน	-	I (only female)
ก.	ได้ข่าว	-	hear, know, get news
ก.,ค.	เสียใจ	-	sorry

น.	เงิน	- money, silver
น.	หน้า	- face, page
น.	สติ	- consciousness
น.	ท้อง	- stomach

☑ Listening exercise

เทิน	เขย	เมย	เจอะ	เชิญ	เลข	เถอะ	เอย
เผย	เคน	เดิน	เฉอ				

Lesson V.V

Exercises for vowel โ-ะ

⊕ แบบฝึกหัดการฟัง

Listen to the cassette carefully, then choose the right word from each pair of words below.

โมะ	มด	คน	โคน	ทน	ทอน	โจบ	จบ
ขบ	ขับ	โล่ง	ล่ง	งง	งน	โถ	ถน
โวย	โว	ยล	โยน	สอน	สน	โดม	ดม

⊕ แบบฝึกหัดการอ่าน

Try to read the following words, then check with the cassette if it is right or not.

ถนน	คนไทย	กฎเกณฑ์	ยากจน
กงศุล	ทดลอง	ตกใจ	พยัญชนะต้น
ผมทอง	ตลก	ขบขัน	เคารพ
อารมณ์	สงสัย	คดโกง	ตัวสะกด
ธงชาติ	รถยนต์	อดทน	ผ้าห่ม

The Thai family

Plan ❶

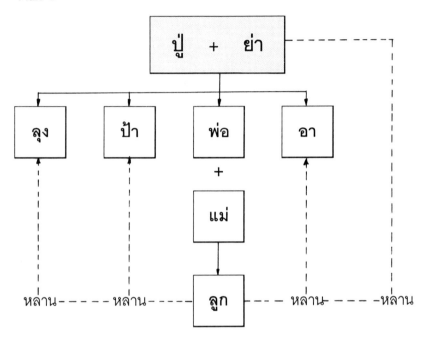

Vocabularies for plan ❶:

On father's side:

น.	ปู่	-	grandfather
น.	ย่า	-	grandmother
น.	ลุง	-	uncle (elder brother of father)
น.	ป้า	-	aunt (elder sister of father)
น.	พ่อ	-	father
น.	อา	-	uncle, aunt (younger brother or sister of father)

Plan ❷

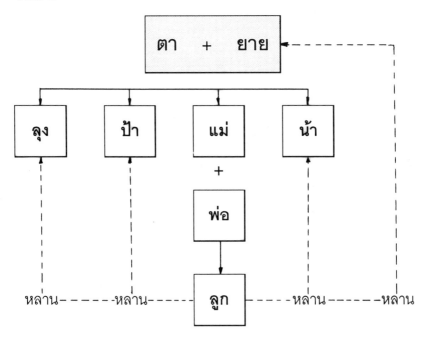

Vocabularies for plan ❷:
On mother's side:

น.	ตา	-	grandfather
น.	ยาย	-	grandmother
น.	ลุง	-	uncle (elder brother of mother)
น.	ป้า	-	aunt (elder sister of mother)
น.	แม่	-	mother
น.	น้า	-	uncle, aunt (younger brother or sister of mother)

Vocabularies for plan ❶ and ❷:

On both father's and mother's side:

น.	ทวด	-	great grandfather or great grandmother
น.	ลูก	-	one's own child
น.	ลูกชาย	-	son
น.	ลูกสาว	-	daughter
น.	หลาน(ชาย)	-	nephew, grandson
น.	หลาน(สาว)	-	niece, granddaughter

Plan ❸

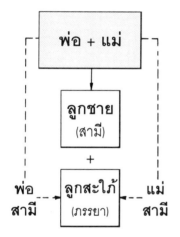

Plan ❹

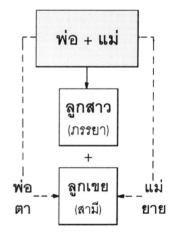

Vocabularies for plan ❸ and ❹:

น.	พ่อสามี	-	father in law (father of the husband)
น.	พ่อตา	-	father in law (father of the wife)
น.	ลูกเขย	-	son in law
น.	แม่สามี	-	mother in law (mother of the husband)
น.	แม่ยาย	-	mother in law (mother of the wife)
น.	ลูกสะใภ้	-	daughter in law

Remark: The parents in law are called like one's own parents. So a son in law calls his wife's father พ่อ.

Plan ❺

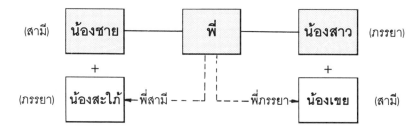

Plan ❻

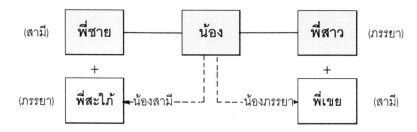

Vocabularies for plan ❺ and ❻:

น.	พี่(ชาย)สามี	-	brother in law (elder brother of the husband)
น.	พี่(สาว)สามี	-	sister in law (elder sister of the husband)
น.	น้อง(ชาย)สามี	-	brother in law (younger brother of the husband)
น.	น้อง(สาว)สามี	-	sister in law (younger sister of the husband)
น.	พี่(ชาย)ภรรยา	-	brother in law (elder brother of the wife)
น.	พี่(สาว)ภรรยา	-	sister in law (elder sister of the wife)
น.	น้อง(ชาย)ภรรยา	-	brother in law (younger brother of the wife)
น.	น้อง(สาว)ภรรยา	-	sister in law (younger sister of the wife)
น.	พี่เขย	-	brother in law (husband of the elder sister)

น.	พี่สะใภ้	- sister in law (wife of the elder brother)
น.	น้องเขย	- brother in law (husband of the younger sister)
น.	น้องสะใภ้	- sister in law (wife of the younger brother)

Remark:

- The age does not have any importance in this group of relatives. Although น้อง means younger relative น้องเขย (husband of younger sister) of Ms. X can be older than her.
- In conversation, one calls the relatives in this group just พี่ or น้อง , more due to the age than to the status. Very often they simply call each other only the first name or nickname, especially when their **ages are** not much different.

Plan ❼

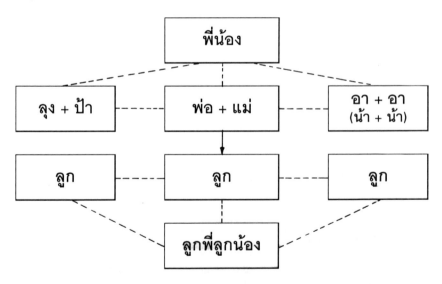

Vocabularies for plan ❼:

| น. | พี่น้อง | - brother(s) and/or **sister(s)** |
| น. | ลูกพี่ลูกน้อง | - cousin |

Remark:

- The wife of ลุง is always called ป้า, like the husband of ป้า is always called ลุง.

- The wife or husband of อา is called อา, like the husband or wife of น้า is called น้า too.

- It is impossible for the Thai to call just the first name of a relative who has a much higher status or who is much older. The title ปู่, ย่า, ตา, ยาย, ลุง, ป้า, น้า or อา is needed as the Thai respect the age or seniority. To be more polite or to show high respect, the word คุณ is put in front of those titles, such as คุณปู่, คุณย่า, etc.

- Among relatives of the same generation such as among brothers and sisters or cousins, sometimes the title พี่ is left out, especially when the ages among them are not much different.

- As the Thai respect the age and the relation among people in Thailand - compared to western societies - is still rather close and warm, the Thai often use the relative titles with those who are in fact non-relatives to demonstrate politeness and friendliness. So it is quite usual to hear someone calling a close friend's mother คุณแม่, a waitress น้อง or an old food vendor ป้า , etc.

⊕ แบบฝึกหัดการอ่าน

วันเกิดของคุณย่า

วันนี้เป็นวันเกิดของคุณย่า ญาติๆทุกคนมาทำบุญเลี้ยงพระที่บ้านของน้ำตาล คุณลุงแสนสุขซึ่งเป็นพี่ชายของคุณพ่อ มากับภรรยาและลูกสาว คือ คุณป้าสมจิตและพี่สุดใจ คุณอาฤทัย น้องสาวของคุณพ่อก็มา

คุณน้าเดือนเพ็ญซึ่งเป็นน้องสาวของคุณแม่ มากับสามีและลูกชาย คือ คุณน้าตะวันกับน้องแมว

ใครๆก็มางานวันเกิดของคุณย่า นอกจากคุณป้าวรรณี เพราะคุณป้าวรรณีซึ่งเป็นพี่สาวของคุณแม่ไปดูงานที่ประเทศญี่ปุ่น

สามพี่น้องคืออนุช น้ำตาลและแตงโมได้เล่นสนุกกับลูกพี่ลูกน้อง คือพี่สุดใจและน้องแมว คุณปู่และคุณย่าก็ดีใจที่ได้พบคุณตาและคุณยาย ครอบ-ครัวไทยเป็นครอบครัวใหญ่ จึงอาจจะวุ่นวายแต่ก็อบอุ่น

Remark: The word ญาติ, like ชาติ, is read without the vowel ิ.

จงตอบคำถามต่อไปนี้

1.ใครเป็นภรรยาของคุณลุงแสนสุข

2.น้องแมวเป็นลูกชายของใคร

3.คุณน้าตะวันคือใคร

4.ทำไมคุณป้าวรรณีไม่มางานวันเกิดของคุณย่า

5.คุณตาเป็นอะไรกับคุณยาย

6.พี่สุดใจเป็นอะไรกับแตงโม

7.คุณพ่อเป็นอะไรกับคุณอาฤทัย

8.คุณแม่เป็นอะไรกับคุณปู่

Vocabulary:

ค.,ก.	ทน	-	patient, durable, to bear
ก.	จบ	-	to end, to finish
ค.	โล่ง	-	clear, open, airy
ก.,ค.,ว.	งง	-	stunned

ก.	โยน	-	throw
ก.	ดม	-	to smell
น.	ถนน	-	road
น.	กฎเกณฑ์	-	rule, regulation
ค.	ยากจน	-	poor (little money)
น.	กงศุล	-	consul
ก.	ทดลอง	-	try out
ก.	ตกใจ	-	frightened
น.	พยัญชนะต้น	-	initial
น.	ผมทอง	-	blond hair
ค.,ว.	ตลก,ขบขัน	-	funny
ก.	เคารพ	-	to respect
น.	อารมณ์	-	mood, emotion
ก.	สงสัย	-	suspect
ก.,ค.,ว.	คดโกง	-	betray, cheat
น.	ตัวสะกด	-	final
น.	ธงชาติ	-	national flag
น.	รถยนต์	-	car
ก.,ค.,ว.	อดทน	-	to be patient
น.	ผ้าห่ม	-	blanket
น.	วันนี้	-	today
น.	ญาติ	-	relatives
ก.	ทำบุญ	-	merit making
ก.	เลี้ยงพระ	-	offer food to monks
ส.	ซึ่ง	-	that, which
ส.	ใครๆ	-	people, everyone
น.	งานวันเกิด	-	birthday celebration
บ.	นอกจาก	-	except
ก.	ไปดูงาน	-	have study tour

น.	(ประเทศ)ญี่ปุ่น	-	Japan
น.	สาม	-	3
ก.,ค.,ว.	ดีใจ	-	glad
ก.	พบ	-	meet, see
ว.	อาจจะ	-	maybe, perhaps
ค.,ว.	วุ่นวาย	-	in disorder
ค.,ว.	อบอุ่น	-	**warm**, sympathetic

☑ Listening exercise

มด   โคน   ทอน   จบ   ขับ   ล่ง   งง   โถ
โวย   ยล   สอน   โดม

☑ Reading exercise

1. คุณป้าสมจิต
2. คุณน้าเดือนเพ็ญกับคุณน้าตะวัน
3. น้องเขยของคุณแม่, สามีของคุณน้าเดือนเพ็ญ, คุณพ่อของน้องแมว
4. คุณป้าวรรณีไปดูงานที่ประเทศญี่ปุ่น
5. สามี
6. ลูกพี่ลูกน้อง
7. พี่ชาย
8. ลูกสะใภ้

Lesson V.VI

Exercises for vowel -อ and -ัว

⊛ แบบฝึกหัดการฟัง

Listen to the cassette carefully, then choose the right word from each pair of words below.

กร	การ	ศน	ศร	นล	นร	วอน	วอ
ออ	อร	ทอน	ทน	จร	จน	ขอ	ขร
รวด	รด	สาย	สวย	ทั่ว	ท่น	มวน	มาน
นวล	นล	หน	หวน	กวง	กาง	วัว	วัน

⊛ แบบฝึกหัดการอ่าน

Try to read the following words, then check with the cassette if it is right or not.

ใจร้อน	อวยพร	บดี	กรณี	มรสุม
ทรมาน	บริษัท	บริโภค	อรวรรณ	ประกวด
สวนผัก	บริจาค	แม่ครัว	มวยไทย	คุณทวด
เจ็บป่วย	ทั่วไป	ปวดฟัน	รถด่วน	ไม้ม้วน

Remark: กรณี can be read both กอ - ระ - ณี and กะ - ระ - ณี.

There are many Thai words which have 2 consonants standing at the beginning. The possibilities about them are:

- leading syllable like in ขยัน, สบาย (see special rules for -ะ) or
- they belong to the special rules for -อ like in บริการ, ทรมาน
- they are what we call อักษรควบกล้ำ (double initials) or อักษรนำ (leading consonants).

In this lesson we will learn อักษรควบกล้ำ.
There are 2 groups of อักษรควบกล้ำ.

1. **อักษรควบแท้** (real double initials). Both consonants share the same vowel and they are pronounced only once together.

    1.1 When ก, ค, ต, ป, ท, พ, บ, ด or ฟ + ร stand at the beginning of a word or syllable:

กร	กรอบ	กรุงเทพฯ	เกรงใจ
คร	ครู	ครอบครัว	ใคร
ตร	เตรียม	ไตร่ตรอง	ตรวจ
ทร	จันทรา	นิทรา	
ปร	ประนีประนอม	ประเทศ	โปรด
พร	พระ	พริก	เพราะ
บร	บราซิล	บรั่นดี	เบรค
ดร	ดรัมเมเยอร์		
ฟร	ฟรี		

Remark: Most words with บร, ดร and ฟร are English.

   1.2 When ก, ค, ป, ผ, พ, บ or ฟ + ล stand at the beginning of a word or syllable:

กล	ไกล	ใกล้	กลอง
คล	คลอง	คลื่น	คล้าย
ปล	ปลอบโยน	เปลี่ยนแปลง	ปลิว
ผล	เผลอไผล	แผลง	ผลีผลาม
พล	พลอย	พลิ้ว	พลาย
บล	บลูยีนส์	บลอนด์	
ฟล	ฟลอริดา	แฟลต	

Remark: Most words with บล and ฟล are English.

1.3 When ก, ข or ค + ว stand at the beginning of a word or syllable.

กว	กว่า	กว้าง	กวาด
ขว	แขวน	ขวน	ขวาย
คว	คว่ำ	ความ	ควาย

2. **อักษรควบไม่แท้** (unreal double initials)

2.1 Only the first consonant is pronounced (mostly with จร, สร, ศร).

จริง   สระผม   สรงน้ำ   ส่งเสริม   ศรัทธา   ประเสริฐ

2.2 ทร is pronounced like ซ.

ทราบ   ทราย   พุทรา   ทรัพย์สิน   ทรุดโทรม   ทรวงอก

Remark: The Thai can pronounce double initials but not double finals. For the words with double finals like มิตร, เพชร, etc. only the first consonant is pronounced.

⊛ แบบฝึกหัดการอ่าน

กลุ้มใจ	เสียขวัญ	เคร่งครัด	ปลากราย	ตรอมตรม
โปรดทราบ	ภัทรา	แพรวพราว	คล่องแคล่ว	ผลัดเปลี่ยน
พลัง	สมุนไพร	ความจริง	เสื่อมทราม	**กรุณา**
โทรศัพท์	พลัดพราก	ความช้าง	ศักดิ์ศรี	กระทรวง

⊛ แบบฝึกหัดการอ่าน

ปีมีสิบสองเดือน

มกราคม	กุมภาพันธ์	มีนาคม	เมษายน
พฤษภาคม	มิถุนายน	กรกฎาคม	สิงหาคม
กันยายน	ตุลาคม	พฤศจิกายน	ธันวาคม

Remark: You must have seen that the months which are ended with ...คม have 31 days and those with ... ยน at the end have 30 days.

การแสดงความคิดเห็นและความรู้สึก
(Opinion and feeling expressions)

ดิฉัน(ไม่)คิดว่า..........		I (don't) think that ...
ผม(ไม่)คาดว่า..........		I (don't) expect that ...
ดิฉัน(ไม่)เชื่อว่า.......	-	I (don't) believe that ...
ผมเดาว่า...........	-	I guess that ...
ผม(ไม่)รู้สึกว่า........	-	I (don't) feel that ...
ผม(ไม่)ชอบ........	-	I (don't) like ...

ดิฉัน(ไม่)สนใจ.........	-	I am (not) interested in …
ดิฉัน(ไม่)เห็นด้วยกับ..ในเรื่อง..	-	I (don't) agree with … about …
ดิฉันชอบ....มากกว่า....	-	I prefer … to …
ทำไม,เพราะอะไร	-	Why?
เพราะ (ว่า) ...	-	Because …

บทสนทนา ❶

สุภา	ทำไมคุณมาเมืองไทยบ่อยคะ	Why do you come to Thailand so often?
จอห์น	เพราะผมชอบเมืองไทยครับ	Because I like Thailand.
สุภา	คุณไม่คิดว่าที่นี่ร้อนมากหรือคะ	Don't you think that it is very hot here?
จอห์น	ร้อนดีกว่าหนาวครับ ผมชอบฤดูร้อนที่นี่มากกว่าฤดูหนาวที่อังกฤษ	Hot is better than cold. I prefer the summer here to the winter in England.

Remark: Can you hear that หรือ and หนาว were pronounced in the rising tone?

บทสนทนา ❷

เย็นจิต	ดิฉันเดาว่าคุณเป็นคนอังกฤษ	I guess that you are British.
ดอริส	เพราะอะไรคะ	Why?

เย็นจิต	เพราะว่ามีแต่ชาวอังกฤษเท่านั้นที่นอนอาบแดดได้ทั้งเดือน	Because there are only the British who can have sunbathing for the whole month.
ดอริส	ดิฉันรู้สึกว่า ผิวสีน้ำตาลทำให้ดิฉันสวยขึ้นค่ะ	I feel that brown skin makes me more beautiful.
เย็นจิต	แต่ดิฉันคิดว่า ผิวขาวสวยกว่านะคะ	But I think that white skin is more beautiful.

Remark:
- The Thai are usually quite different from "creatures of habit", especially during holidays. They like new things. To be in one place for longer than 3 - 4 days is normally out of question for them.
- As the Thai have healthy brown skin which may vary from very light to rather dark brown, many of them have trend to think that whiter skin is more beautiful. Human beings are not easily satisfied, are they?

Vocabulary:

ก.	วอน	-	beg
ก.	ทอน	-	change
ก.	ขอ	-	beg, ask for
ก.	รด	-	pour
ค.,ว.	ทั่ว, ทั่วไป	-	everywhere, in general
ค.	ใจร้อน	-	hot tempered
ก.	อวยพร	-	wish luck to someone
น.	กรณี	-	case
น.	มรสุม	-	monsoon

ก.	ทรมาน	-	torture
น.	บริษัท	-	company
ก.	บริโภค	-	consume
ก.	ประกวด	-	contest
น.	สวนผัก	-	vegetable plantation
ก.	บริจาค	-	donate
น.	แม่ครัว	-	female cook
น.	มวยไทย	-	Thai boxing
ก.	เจ็บป่วย	-	to be ill
ก.	ปวดฟัน	-	to have toothache
น.	รถด่วน	-	express train- or bus
น.	ไม้ม้วน	-	the vowel "ใ"
ค.	กรอบ	-	crispy
น.	กรุงเทพฯ	-	Bangkok
ก.,ค.	เกรงใจ	-	the feeling not to make problems to anyone
ก.	เตรียม	-	to prepare
ก.	ไตร่ตรอง	-	consider
ก.	ตรวจ	-	to control
ก.	ประนีประนอม	-	to compromise
น.	พระ(สงฆ์)	-	monk
น.	พริก	-	chilli
น.	บราซิล	-	Brazil
น.	บรั่นดี	-	brandy
ก.	เบรค	-	to brake
น.	ดรัมเมเยอร์	-	drum major
ค.,ว.	ฟรี	-	free
ค.,ว.	ไกล	-	far (distance)
ค.,ว.	ใกล้	-	near (distance)

น.	กลอง	-	drum
น.	คลอง	-	canal
น.	คลื่น	-	wave
ค.,ว.	คล้าย	-	to be similar to
ก.	ปลอบโยน	-	soothe
ก.	เปลี่ยนแปลง	-	to change
ก.	ปลิว	-	blow away with the wind
ก.,ว.	เผลอไผล	-	unconsciously
ก.,ว.	แผลง	-	strange, to change
ก.,ว.	ผลีผลาม	-	hasty
น.	พลอย	-	gemstone
ก.	พลิ้ว	-	blow in the wind
น.	พลาย	-	male elephant
ว.	กว่า	-	more than (comparative degree), till
ค.,ว.	กว้าง	-	wide
ก.	กวาด	-	sweep
ก.	แขวน	-	hang
ก.	ขวนขวาย	-	try hard
ก.	คว่ำ	-	turn upside down
น.	ความ	-	prefix which is followed by an adjective or verb, and makes the word a noun.
ก.	สระผม	-	wash the hair
ก.	สรงน้ำ	-	give shower to Buddha image
ก.	ส่งเสริม	-	support
น.	ศรัทธา	-	faith
ก.	ทราบ	-	know (very polite)
น.	ทราย	-	sand
น.	พุทรา	-	a kind of Thai fruit
น.	ทรัพย์สิน	-	property

ก.,ค.	ทรุดโทรม	-	ruin
น.	ทรวงอก	-	chest
ก.	กลุ้มใจ	-	worry
ก.	เสียขวัญ	-	demoralized
ก.,ค.,ว.	เคร่งครัด	-	strict
น.	ปลากราย	-	a kind of river fish
ก.,ค.,ว.	ตรอมตรม	-	grieve
	โปรดทราบ	-	attention, please!
ค.,ว.	แพรวพราว	-	glittering, brilliant
ค.,ว.	คล่องแคล่ว	-	fluent
ก.	ผลัดเปลี่ยน	-	change, exchange, turn
น.	พลัง	-	power, energy
น.	สมุนไพร	-	herb
น.	ความจริง	-	truth, reality
ก.,ค.,ว.	เสื่อมทราม	-	decline
ก.,น.	โทรศัพท์	-	telephone
ก.	พลัดพราก	-	separate
น.	ควานช้าง	-	elephant trainer
น.	ศักดิ์ศรี	-	pride, dignity
น.	กระทรวง	-	ministry
น.	สิบสอง	-	12
น.	มกราคม	-	January
น.	กุมภาพันธ์	-	February
น.	มีนาคม	-	March
น.	เมษายน	-	April
น.	พฤษภาคม	-	May
น.	มิถุนายน	-	June
น.	กรกฎาคม	-	July
น.	สิงหาคม	-	August

น.	กันยายน	-	September
น.	ตุลาคม	-	October
น.	พฤศจิกายน	-	November
น.	ธันวาคม	-	December
น.	ฤดูร้อน	-	summer
น.	ฤดูฝน	-	rainy season
น.	ฤดูหนาว	-	winter
น.	อากาศกำลังสบาย	-	mild weather
ก.	แสดง	-	show, demonstrate
น.	ความคิดเห็น	-	opinion
น.	ความรู้สึก	-	feeling
ก.	คาด, คาดหมาย	-	expect
ก.	เชื่อ	-	believe
ก.	รู้สึก	-	feel
ก.	สนใจ	-	interested in
ก.	เห็นด้วย	-	agree
ค.	หนาว	-	cold
ค.	ทั้ง...,ทั้งหมด	-	all
น.	ผิว	-	skin
น.	สีน้ำตาล	-	brown
ค.	สวยขึ้น	-	more beautiful

☑ Listening exercise

กร	ศน	นล	วอน	ออ	ทน	จร	ขอ	รวด
สาย	ทั่ว	มวน	นวล	หน	กาง	วัน		

Lesson VI

กฎการผันเสียงวรรณยุกต์
Rules of Tones

To be able to master the rules of tones in Thai language, you need to know how the Thai divide their consonants into 3 groups. Please look back at lesson I, page 21.

Then there are คำเป็น and คำตาย (open / closed syllables) which can help you to use the rules of tones more efficiently.

Anyway the most important thing is that you must be able to distinguish and pronounce the 5 tones correctly. If you need more practices, just go back to lesson III, page 33.

Now we will firstly get to know คำเป็น and คำตาย.

คำเป็น (open syllable) is a syllable that you can pronounce long without any difficulty. There are:

❶ long syllables without any final, such as ตา, ปู่, สี่, แม่, เสื้อ, ใจ

❷ all syllables with final อ, ง, น, ณ, ร, ล, ฬ, ญ, ม, ย or ว (they have the sounds of o, ng, n, m, i or u in English), such as พ่อ, ทอง, คุณ, ขม, ยาย, หิว

คำตาย (closed syllable) is a syllable that you can not pronounce long. There are:

❶ short syllables without any final, e.g. กะทิ, ดุ, เกาะ

❷ all syllables with final ก, ข, ค, ฆ, จ, ช, ด, ฎ, ต, ฏ, ฐ, ถ, ท, ธ, ฌ, ส, ศ, ษ, บ, ป, พ, ภ or ฟ (they have the sounds of k, t, and p in English), such as หัก, ปิด, ตรวจ, จบ

On the next page you can see a table which shows the rules of tones.

▨▨▨ shows the basic tones of each group of consonants. This means the basic tone of the high consonants is the rising tone, of the middle and low consonants are the middle tone.

Now let's study the **high and middle consonants** first because both groups have easy and practical rules.

▨▨▨ shows that the tone sounds of the syllables within it are according to the tone marks. So when you see a syllable with an initial from these 2 groups with any tone mark, just read it from what you see, such as ข่า must have the low tone sound, จ๊ะ must have the high tone sound.

The syllables out of the 2 screen blocks show that any **closed syllable without tone mark** of which the initial is a high or middle consonant has always the low tone sound, such as ฝาก or จะ.

The real problem maker is the third group: the low consonants. When any consonant of this group is the initial of an opened syllable, with low tone mark, it is pronounced with the falling tone sound. With falling tone mark, it is pronounced with the high tone sound. Let's say its tone sound is always one step higher than its tone mark.

TONE SOUNDS	OPEN SYLLABLES					CLOSED SYLLABLES				
	middle	low	falling	high	rising	middle	low	falling	high	rising
High consonants (10) ข ฃ ฉ ฐ ถ ผ ฝ ศ ษ ส ห		ข่า ขว่า ขื่อ	ข้า ขว้า ขื้อ	ข๊า ขว๊า ขื๊อ	ขา ขวา ขอ		ขาก ขด ขวะ	ข้าก ข้ด ขว้ะ	ข๊าก ข๊ด ขว๊ะ	ข๋าก ข๋ด ขว๋ะ
Middle consonants (9) ก จ ฎ ฏ ด ต บ ป อ	กา กรู เอา	ก่า กรู่ เอ่า	ก้า กรู้ เอ้า	ก๊า กรู๊ เอ๊า	ก๋า กรู๋ เอ๋า		กาก กด เอาะ	ก้าก ก้ด เอ้าะ	ก๊าก ก๊ด เอ๊าะ	ก๋าก ก๋ด เอ๋าะ
Low consonants (23) ค ฅ ฆ ง ช ซ ฌ ญ ฑ ฒ ณ ท ธ น พ ฟ ภ ม ย ร ล ว ฬ ฮ	คา เคา		ค่า เค่า	ค้า เค้า				แคบ แคน	แคน คาบ คีด	แคบ คาบ คีด	แคบ คาบ คีด

Keys of symbols: ▨ basic tone   ☐ tone mark = tone sound   ☐ tone mark ≠ tone sound

In the case that the initial of a closed syllable is a low consonant, there are unfortunately many possibilities:

❶ When it has the rising tone mark, it is also pronounced with the rising tone sound, such as แย๋ก or ค๋ะ.

❷ When a close syllable has a long vowel and a final but without a tone mark, it is pronounced with the falling tone sound, such as แยก. However, when such a syllable has the falling tone mark, it is pronounced with the high tone sound, such as ค้าบ.

❸ When a closed syllable has a short vowel but no tone mark, it is pronounced with the high tone sound, such as นะ or วัด.

❹ When a closed syllable has a short vowel with the low tone mark, it is pronounced with the falling tone sound, such as น่ะ or วั่ด.

From the table you can see that only the opened syllables which have middle consonants as the initial can have all 5 tones. So the table can also help your writing, such as it is absolutely wrong to write ค๊ะ or นี๊ะ which are very common mistakes made by many Thais.

The rules of tones are really complicated, aren't they? Please do not feel discouraged. Study the table with explanation slowly and carefully a few times, then you will master them. After this lesson, you can be sure that you can read or pronounce almost every word in this tonal language so correctly that even the Thai will definitely feel surprised.

แบบฝึกหัดการออกเสียง

If you are not sure, use the table (it can also help you to understand the rules better), then check your pronunciation with the cassette.

ขาด	ฉัน	ฐาน	ถิ่น	ผึ้ง	ฝ้า	ศีล	ษิต
สูง	หาก	เกิน	จิ๋ม	เด็ก	ตาย	บี้	ป่วย
อ่อน	คน	ฌาต	ง่าย	ช้าง	ซ้าย	ยาด	เฌร
ฑล	เฒ่า	ธัก	แท้	นิ่ม	พัด	แฟบ	มาก
ยักษ์	ร้าว	ว่าน	ภพ	ฮูก	ล่อ	คุ้ย	งัด

Vocabulary:

น.	ทอง	-	gold
ค.	ขม	-	bitter
ก.	หิว	-	hungry
ก.	หัก	-	break
ก.,ค.	ปิด	-	to close
ค.	ขาด	-	torn
ส.	ฉัน	-	I
น.	ฐาน	-	basement
น.,ค.	ถิ่น	-	local, domestic
น.	ผึ้ง	-	bee
น.	ฝ้า	-	bremish
น.	ศีล	-	religious precept, commandment
สัน.	หาก	-	if
ค.	เกิน	-	over
น.,ค.	เด็ก	-	child, young
ค.	อ่อน	-	young, soft, gentle

น.,ค.	เฒ่า	-	old
ค.	นิ่ม	-	soft
น.,ก.	พัด	-	fan, blow
น.	ยักษ์	-	giant
ก.,ค.	ร้าว	-	crack
น.	ว่าน	-	a kind of plants
ก.	คุ้ย	-	dig
ก.	งัด	-	force open

Lesson VII

อักษรนำ
Leading Consonant

Do you still remember อักษรควบกล้ำ (Double Initials) from lesson V.VI?

A word or syllable with a leading consonant also has two consonants standing at the beginning but they are differently pronounced.

To be able to use the rules of the leading consonant, you need to know the 3 consonant groups (lesson I, page 21) and understand the rules of tones from the last lesson very well.

The rules of the leading consonant:

❶ อ + ย: There are, due to this rule, only 4 words: อย่า, อยู่, อย่าง and อยาก. อ is not pronounced but the words (which have ย as initial) have the tone sound as if อ were their initial. For example: In the word อย่า, อ is not pronounced and ย่า alone has falling tone while อ่า has low tone, when they are combined to be one word อย่า is pronounced "YA" with the low tone.

❷ ห + a single consonant (ง, ญ, ณ, น, ย, ม, ร, ล, ว, ฬ): ห is not pronounced but the words (which have a single consonant as initial), have the tone sound as if ห were their initial. For example: In the word ไหม: ห is not pronounced and ไม alone has middle tone while ไห has rising tone, so ไหม is pronounced "MAI" with the rising tone.

The words with a leading consonant from the rules 3 - 7 are pronounced as if they had -ะ.

❸ **A high consonant (ข, ฉ, ฐ, ถ, ผ, ฝ, ส, ศ, ษ,) + a single consonant:**
The high consonant is pronounced as if it had -ะ and the single consonant which is the word's initial is pronounced as if it were a high consonant. For example: The word สยาม is pronounced "SA + YAM" (with the rising tone).

❹ **A middle consonant (ก, จ, ด, ฎ, ต, ฏ, บ, ป, อ) + a single consonant:**
The middle consonant is pronounced as if it had -ะ and the single consonant which is the word's initial is pronounced as if it were a middle consonant. For example: ตลาด is pronounced "DTA + LAD" (with the low tone).

❺ **A high consonant + a twin consonant (ค, ฅ, ช, ซ, ฌ, ฑ, ฒ, ท, ธ, พ, ฟ, ภ, ฮ):** The high consonant is pronounced as if it had -ะ and the twin consonant which is the word's initial is pronounced with its normal tone. For example: สภา is pronounced "SA + PA" (with the middle tone).

❻ **A high consonant + a middle consonant:** The high consonant is pronounced as if it had -ะ and the middle consonant which is the word's initial is pronounced with its normal tone. For example: สบาย is pronounced "SA + BAI" (with the middle tone).

❼ **A low consonant + any consonant:** The low consonant is pronounced as if it had -ะ and the other consonant which is the word's initial is pronounced with its normal tone. For example: พยาน is pronounced "PA + YAN (with the middle tone).

Let's say the leading consonant, due to the conditions of the rules 1 - 4, controls the tone of the word's initial whereas it - due to the conditions of the rules 5 - 7 - does not have such an influence over the initial at all.

⊕ แบบฝึกหัดการออกเสียง

If you are not sure, study the rules once again (it can also help you to understand them better), then check your pronunciation with the cassette.

อยาก	หรือ	ผนัง	อนึ่ง	เผชิญ	ขบวน
หนอน	ตลิ่ง	สลัด	ขยะ	แสดง	ไหน
รหัส	พยาน	หน้า	องุ่น	ชฎา	พยาบาล
หญิง	อภัย	สวรรค์	ถนัด	สมุน	พยายาม

การขอร้อง (Request)

In order to request politely and formally, โปรด or กรุณา is usually put in front of an imperative. For example:

โปรดข้ามถนนตรงทางม้าลาย	**Please** cross the road at the zebra crossing.
รถช้า: **โปรด**ขับชิดซ้าย	Slow vehicles: **Please** keep left!
กรุณางดสูบบุหรี่	**Please** do not smoke!

Both กรุณา and โปรด are more often used in the written language than in the spoken. In a conversation they sound very formal and are not used with the younger or those with a lower status. The Thai have in fact several ways of making a polite request when they lead a daily conversation. For example:

(ดิฉัน)ขอน้ำส้มสองแก้วค่ะ	I would like to have two glasses of orange juice, **please**.
(ดิฉัน)ขอโทรศัพท์ไปประเทศอังกฤษ	I would like to call to England, **please**.

The Thai say ขอ when they politely order food, drink, or ask to do something. ได้ไหม is often put at the end of the request in order to make it even more polite.

(ดิฉัน)**ขอ**แลกเงินยี่สิบบาท**ได้ไหม**คะ	Can I change a 20 Baht bank note, **please**?
ขอพริกป่นหน่อย**ได้ไหม**คะ	May I have a little bit chilli powder, **please**?

When the Thai politely ask someone to do something for them, they will just put ช่วย at the beginning and หน่อยได้ไหม at the end of an imperative.

อากาศหนาวมาก	It is very cold.
ช่วยปิดหน้าต่าง**หน่อยได้ไหม**คะ	**Can** you **please** close the window?
ผมไม่เข้าใจคำนี้	I don't understand this word.
ช่วยอธิบาย**หน่อยได้ไหม**ครับ	**Can** you **please** explain me?

Remark:

There are still some more words that one can use in a request:

วาน is almost the same as ช่วย but it is more informal and it can not be used with the much older people or those with a higher status as it has a little bit tone of order. For example:

วานเช็ดโต๊ะให้(ผม)**หน่อย**	**Please** clean the table (for me).

ขอให้ is very similar to โปรด and กรุณา but it is more often used in the spoken language. For examples:

ขอให้ฟังผมบ้างได้ไหม	**Can** you **please** listen to me?
ขอให้ผมไปด้วยนะครับ	**Please** let me go with (you).

ขอให้ can be also used in wishing someone something. For example:

ขอให้คุณมีความสุขตลอดไป   (I) **wish** you an eternal happiness.

ขอได้โปรด, ขอได้โปรดกรุณา are the utmost humble request. An exaggeration to give you an imagination of the way a Thai uses the phrases is that he almost knees down in front of his conversation partner when he asks that person to do something for him. For example:

ขอได้โปรดเข้าใจผมบ้าง   **Could** you **please** understand me a
เถอะครับ   little bit?

By the way, the Thai have many particles to soften their informal request. They are หน่อย, นะ, บ้าง, ที, เถิด, เถอะ etc. You can simply put one among them at the end of the sentence.

การเปรียบเทียบ (Comparison)
การเปรียบเทียบขั้นเสมอกัน (Positive degree)

To compare things or people who are the same or equal is easy. เท่ากับ or เท่ากัน is needed to say that, e.g.

ทัศนีย์อายุ 30 ปี   Tasani is 30 years old.
สมใจอายุ 30 ปี   Somjai is 30 years old.
ทัศนีย์อายุ**เท่ากับ**สมใจ   Tasani is **as** old **as** Somjai. *or*
ทัศนีย์และสมใจอายุ**เท่ากัน**   Tasani and Somjai have **the same** age.

To compare an extreme similarity **เหมือนกับ** or **เหมือนกัน** is needed.

มุกกับมนเป็นพี่น้องฝาแฝด   Muk and Mon are twins.
มุกมีหน้าตา**เหมือนกับ**มน   Muk looks **the same as** Mon. *or*
มุกและมนมีหน้าตา**เหมือนกัน**   Muk and Mon look **the same**.

When the degree of similarity is less คล้ายกับ or คล้ายกัน is needed.

พิมเป็นลูกสาวของคุณประไพ	Pim is Mrs. Bprapai's daughter.
พิมมีหน้าตา**คล้ายกับ**คุณแม่ของเธอ	Pim looks **similar to** her mother. *or*
หน้าตาของคุณประไพและพิม**คล้ายกัน**	Mrs. Bprapai and Pim look **similar to each** other.

To talk about the same person or the same thing, we use เดียวกับ or เดียวกัน.

จอห์นมาจากอังกฤษ	John came from England.
ริชาร์ดมาจากอังกฤษ	Richard came from England.
จอห์นมาจากประเทศ**เดียวกับ**ริชาร์ด	John came from **the same** country **as** Richard. *or*
จอห์นและริชาร์ดมาจากประเทศ**เดียวกัน**	John and Richard came from **the same** country.

Remark:

You should have seen by now the difference between กับ and กัน. We use กับ and กัน only when we mention about at least two persons or two things (not only in comparison) but กับ must be followed by a noun or pronoun. For examples:

ผมไปตลาด**กับ**คุณ	I go the market **with** you.
เราไปตลาด**ด้วยกัน**	We go the market **together**.
คุณจะไปตลาด	You will go the market.
ผมก็จะไปตลาด**เหมือนกัน**	I will **also** go to the market.
ผมก็จะไปตลาด**เหมือนกับ**คุณ	I will **also** go to the market **like you**.

การเปรียบเทียบขั้นกว่า (Comparative degree)

Comparative degree in Thai is a little bit more complicated than in English.

- ❶ Between 2 things or 2 people, simply put กว่า behind the adjective or adverb.

สุภาสวย	Supa is beautiful.
วรรณีสวยมาก	Wanni is very beautiful.
วรรณีสวย**กว่า**สุภา	Wanni is **more** beautiful **than** Supa.
วิชัยมีเงิน	Wichai has money.
ดุสิตมีเงินมาก	Dusit has much money.
ดุสิตมีเงิน**มากกว่า**วิชัย	Dusit has **more** money **than** Wichai.
นิดาทำงานดี	Nida works well.
ศิริทำงานดีมาก	Siri works very well.
ศิริทำงาน**ดีกว่า**นิดา	Siri works **better than** Nida.

- ❷ The same person or thing in 2 different times or situations.

ปีก่อนสุภาสูง 160 เซนติเมตร	Last year Supa was 160 cm tall.
ปีนี้เขาสูง 162 เซนติเมตร	This year she is 162 cm tall.
ปีนี้สุภา**สูงขึ้น**(กว่าเมื่อปีก่อน)	This year Supa is **taller** (**than** last year).
เมื่อวานนี้อากาศดี	Yesterday the weather was good.
วันนี้อากาศไม่ดี	Today the weather is bad.
วันนี้อากาศ**เลวลง**(กว่าเมื่อวาน)	Today the weather is **worse** (**than** yesterday).

In this case you have to consider the meaning of the adjective or adverb of which direction it is. When the direction of the meaning is towards increasing or developing (more, better, ...), we use ... ขึ้น. On the contrary when it indicates decreasing or decline, we use ... ลง. For example:

ดีขึ้น	≠	เลวลง	better	≠	worse
มากขึ้น	≠	น้อยลง	more	≠	less
อ้วนขึ้น	≠	ผอมลง	fatter	≠	thinner
แก่ขึ้น	≠	เด็กลง	older	≠	younger
ฉลาดขึ้น	≠	โง่ลง	more intelligent	≠	more stupid

การเปรียบเทียบขั้นสุด (Superlative degree)

The superlative degree is very easy. Just put ที่สุด behind the adjective or adverb. For example:

นิดสูง 150 ซ.ม.	Nid is 150 cm tall.
น้อยสูง 155 ซ.ม.	Noi is 155 cm tall.
หนูสูง 160 ซ.ม.	Nu is 160 cm tall.
ในบรรดาเด็กทั้ง 3 คน หนู**สูงที่สุด**	Among all 3 children, Nu is **the tallest**.

Remark:

more than 2 kg's	**มาก**กว่า 2 กิโลกรัม or 2 กิโลกรัม**กว่า**
longer than 2 km's	**ยาว**กว่า 2 กิโลเมตร or 2 กิโลเมตร**กว่า**
the **more** ... the ...**er**	ยิ่ง...ยิ่ง...

For example:

    the **more** it is, the **better** it is   **ยิ่ง**มาก**ยิ่ง**ดี

too ...	เกินไป

For example:

too much	มาก**เกินไป**
too ... to ...	......เกินกว่าที่จะ.....

For example:

too beautiful **to** be real	สวยเกินกว่าที่จะเป็นความจริง

Vocabulary:

	อย่า	-	do not
น.	อย่าง	-	type
ว.	อย่าง....	-	prefix to form an adverb out of an adjective (e.g. ดี ⇨ อย่างดี)
ก.	อยาก	-	want, like to
น.	สยาม	-	Siam
น.	ตลาด	-	market
น.	สภา	-	parliament
น.	พยาน	-	witness
น.	ผนัง	-	wall
ว.	อนึ่ง	-	by the way (written language)
ก.	เผชิญ	-	meet, confront
น.	ขบวน	-	parade, classifier for รถไฟ (train)
น.	หนอน	-	worm
น.	ตลิ่ง	-	shore
น.	สลัด	-	salad
น.	ขยะ	-	garbage
ว.	ไหน	-	which
น.	รหัส	-	code

น.	องุ่น	-	grape
น.	ชฎา	-	crown
น.	พยาบาล	-	nurse, take care of a patient
น.,ค.	หญิง	-	woman, girl, female
ก.	อภัย, ให้อภัย	-	forgive
น.	สวรรค์	-	paradise
ก.	พยายาม	-	try to do
ก.	ข้าม	-	cross
ค.,ว.	ตรง	-	straight, at, on
น.	ทางม้าลาย	-	zebra crossing
ค.,ว.	ช้า	-	slow
ค.,ว.,บ.	ชิด	-	to, on, to be close to
ค.	ซ้าย	-	left
ก.	งด	-	stop
ก.	สูบ	-	smoke
น.	บุหรี่	-	cigarette
ก.	ขอ	-	to ask for something
น.	น้ำส้ม	-	orange juice
น.	แก้ว	-	glass
น.	พริกป่น	-	chilli powder
ก.	ช่วย	-	help
น.	หน้าต่าง	-	window
ก.	อธิบาย	-	explain
ก.	เช็ด	-	to clean
น.	ความสุข	-	happiness
ค.,ว.	ตลอดไป	-	forever, eternal
ก.	เปรียบเทียบ	-	compare
น.	(พี่น้อง)ฝาแฝด	-	twins
น.	หน้าตา	-	face, appearance

น.	ปีก่อน	- last year
น.	ปีนี้	- this year
ค.,ว.	เลว	- bad
ค.	อ้วน	- fat
ค.	ผอม	- thin
ค.	ฉลาด	- intelligent, clever
ค.	โง่	- stupid

Lesson VIII

สรรพนามและนาม
Pronoun and Noun

Pronoun (สรรพนาม)

Thanks to the Thai culture, the pronoun in Thai language is a complicated issue. To be able to use a suitable pronoun, one needs to consider the age, sex, relationship, social status, etc. of one's self and of the conversation partner. A wrong or unsuitable pronoun can lead to misunderstanding, impoliteness, improperness or even offending.

There are really a lot of pronouns in Thai. This book will show you only those you should need or hear rather often.

❶ The first singular personal pronoun (I):

For women and girls:	ฉัน,ดิฉัน,หนู,ข้าพเจ้า,เรา,พี่,น้อง
For men and boys:	ฉัน,ผม,กระผม,ข้าพเจ้า,เรา,พี่

For a rather formal conversation or among non acquaintances, the most common and widely used pronoun for women and girls (from the age of 15 years onward) is ดิฉัน. หนู is more suitable for girls especially those under 15.

In an informal conversation with the elder or those with a higher status, ดิฉัน and หนู remain the most suitable pronouns although many choose to call themselves by using their nicknames instead. น้อง is also common when the speaker regards herself as a younger sister of her conversation partner.

although they are not real relatives. As mentioned before, the Thai respect the age and seniority.

The best pronoun for men and boys in almost all cases is ผม. กระผม is very formal and extremely polite. Actually men use กระผม only with monks and much older people or those with a very much higher status.

ฉัน and เรา are commonly used by both women and men from all ages in an informal conversation between acquaintances with similar age and status or with the younger or those who have a lower status.

ข้าพเจ้า is an extraordinarily formal word. The chance to use this word is more often in an official or very formal speech or writing. In that case it is good for both women and men.

พี่ can also be used by the people of both genders and every age. Thai use this pronoun very often in an informal conversation. The point is that the speaker must be older than the conversation partner. Many husbands call themselves พี่ when they talk with their wives. The words พี่ and น้อง the Thai use with non-relatives just reflect the intimacy, friendliness, care and respect they have for each other.

❷ **The first plural personal pronoun (we):** เรา or พวกเรา

This pronoun is easy. The use is not different from its counterpart in English.

❸ **The second singular personal pronoun (you):** เธอ, คุณ, เจ้า, หนู, ท่าน

The most often used word is คุณ. คุณ is always polite for people of both genders at almost every age, status, and for almost all kinds of relationship.

ท่าน is very polite and formal. The Thai use ท่าน only with those who are much older and more often with those who have really much higher status.

เธอ is more used with the younger people or those with lower status. It is possible to here this word among friends, too.

หนู and เจ้า are used with the younger people (when they do not have higher status). Normally older people use this word to show kindness and intimacy to the younger.

Please note that it is very common (and polite) for a Thai to use relative titles instead of "you" both with relatives and non-relatives. For example: when a man asks his aunt or a non-relative, who looks older than his mother, where she is going to, he will probably say **ป้าจะไปไหนครับ**, not **คุณ**จะไปไหนครับ.

❹ **The second plural personal pronoun (you):** (พวก)คุณ, (พวก)ท่าน, (พวก)เธอ, (พวก)หนู

The use of these pronouns is the same as point ❸. The word พวก is added in front just to stress that they are more than 1 person but it is not really needed.

❺ **The third singular personal pronoun (he, she, it):** เขา,เธอ, ท่าน,แก,หล่อน,มัน

เขา is generally used for "he" and "she". Anyway for "she" เธอ even sounds more beautiful. แก can be used for children and old people but for very formal conversation, in order to show utmost respect, ท่าน is the right word for older people or those with a higher status. Some people use หล่อน for "she" but it does not sound really nice, so although you may hear or read it, avoid using this word yourself. มัน is used only for things and animals. Although you may hear some Thai using มัน with close friends or young relatives in a very informal conversation, it is better for you not to use this word with human beings at all because in fact it does not sound polite.

❻ **The third plural personal pronoun (they):** (พวก)เขา, (พวก)มัน, (พวก)ท่าน

Again, the word พวก is not really needed and the use of these pronouns is not different from point ❺.

❼ **Indefinite pronoun (one, everyone, -body, -thing, all, each, etc.)**

    for human beings: ใคร, ใครๆ, บางคน, ทุกคน , for example:

ทุกคนต้องตาย	Everyone must die.
บางคนกลัวความมืด	Some people are afraid of darkness.
ไม่มีใครเกลียดเงิน	No one hates money.
ใครๆก็ต้องการงานดี	Everyone wants good jobs.

Remark: ทุกคน และ ใครๆ have the sense of plural.

    for things: บางสิ่ง(บางอย่าง), ทุกสิ่ง(ทุกอย่าง), อะไร, อะไรๆ, e.g.

บางสิ่งบางอย่างเปลี่ยนไป	Something has changed.
ทุกสิ่งทุกอย่างเหมือนเดิม	Everything is the same.
ผมชอบบางสิ่งที่นั่น	I like something there.
ฉันรักทุกอย่างที่ภูเก็ต	I love everything in Phuket.
อะไรๆก็ดี	Everything is good.
ขอผมกินอะไรหน่อย	Let me eat something.

Remark: บางสิ่ง(บางอย่าง), ทุกสิ่ง(ทุกอย่าง), อะไรๆ have the sense of plural.

❽ **Demonstrative pronoun (this, that, these, those):** นี่, นั่น, โน่น, ที่นี่, ที่นั่น, ที่โน่น

When the person or the thing we talk about is near นี่ is used. นั่น indicates that the distance between that person or thing and us is longer. โน่น has the sense of "over there". For example:

นี่คือบ้านของฉัน นั่นคือร้านขายขนมปัง และโน่นคือโรงภาพยนต์

This (here) is my house, that (there) is the bakery and overthere is the cinema.

Remark: นี้, นั้น, โน้น have the same meanings like นี่, นั่น, โน่น but they are adjectives and in most cases a classification noun is needed. For example:

ผมรักผู้หญิงคน**นี้**	I love **this** woman.	(คน is classification noun for human beings)
เขาจะซื้อรถคัน**นั้น**	He will buy **that** car.	(คัน is classification noun for cars)
ตึกหลัง**โน้น**เก่า	The building **over there** is old.	(หลัง is classification noun for buildings)

❾ Relative pronoun (that, which, who, what ...): ที่, ซึ่ง, อัน

A relative pronoun is used in a relative sentence. For example:

ใครๆก็ชอบฤดูร้อน**ซึ่ง**มีอากาศอบอุ่น	Everyone likes summer **which** has warm weather.
เธอมีดวงตา**ที่**สวยมาก	She has eyes **which** are very beautiful.
ฉันไม่เคยเสียใจ**ที่**แต่งงานกับผู้ชายคนนี้	I have never been regret **that** I am married to this man.
ประเทศไทยคือบ้านเกิดเมืองนอน**อัน**เป็นที่รักยิ่งของฉัน	Thailand is my home country **which** is so much beloved to me.

Remark: ที่ and ซึ่ง can be generally used in the same way. อัน is more used in beautiful written language.

Different from English, Thai is not an inflectional but an isolating language. Thus, the forms of words never change, such as ผม always remains ผม, no matter it means I or me.

Noun (นาม)

As explained before, nouns in Thai never change their forms due to genders, numbers, or anything. So there is in general not much to discuss about it. However there are two kinds of nouns which must be learned. They are ลักษณนาม and สมุหนาม.

ลักษณนาม (Classification noun)

Classification nouns are needed and there are really many of them in Thai language. This book will anyway give you only those which are often used in daily life.

How to use classification nouns is also rather complicated. Here are the rules:

❶ Classification nouns stand **behind the number**.

	นาม (noun)	จำนวน (number)	ลักษณนาม (classification noun)
two blouses	เสื้อ	สอง	ตัว
one teacher	ครู	หนึ่ง	คน

❷ Classification nouns stand **in front of the word which means "one"**.

	นาม	ลักษณนาม	"one"
one man	ชาย	คน	หนึ่ง
the only child	ลูก	คน	เดียว
one cat	แมว	ตัว	เดียว

❸ Classification nouns stand **in front of the ordinal number or word**.

	นาม	ลักษณนาม	ลำดับที่ (ordinal number or word)
the first son	ลูกชาย	คน	แรก
the last daughter	ลูกสาว	คน	สุดท้อง
the eldest brother	พี่ชาย	คน	โต

English	นาม	ลักษณนาม	คุณศัพท์
the youngest sister	น้องสาว	คน	เล็ก
the first house	บ้าน	หลัง	ที่หนึ่ง
the last love	ความรัก	ครั้ง	สุดท้าย
the third meal	อาหาร	มื้อ	ที่สาม

❹ Classification nouns stand **in front of the adjective**.

English	นาม	ลักษณนาม	คุณศัพท์ (adjective)
this car	รถ	คัน	นี้
that child	เด็ก	คน	นั้น
the beloved woman	สาว	คน	รัก
the green pen	ปากกา	ด้าม	เขียว
the sharp knife	มีด	เล่ม	คม

Classification nouns which are often used in daily conversation.

Classification nouns	for
ตัว	animal, furniture, clothes, photo camera
ข้าง(1), คู่(2)	shoes, socks, earrings, chop-sticks
ใบ	hat, bag, fruit, egg, dish, bowl, cup, glass, business card, card, bank note
ขวด	bottle
คัน	car, truck, bus, bicycle, motorbike, spoon, fork, umbrella
ลำ	boat, ship, aircraft
ขบวน	train, tram, subway, parade
เล่ม	knife, copy book, book, scissors, needle, candle
คน	human being
ผืน	fabric, mat, carpet, piece of land

แผ่น	paper, disk, wood slice, tile
วง	ring, music group
สาย	street, way, canal, river, airline, bus
เส้น	thread, robe, hair, noodle
หลัง	house, building, cottage, tent, castle, piano
ซอง	pack of cigarettes, envelope
บาน	door, window, mirror, picture frame
ดวง	star, bulb, stamp
ต้น	tree, pile, log
ฉบับ	letter, telegram, magazine
รูป	picture. photo
เรื่อง	novel, story, tale
บท	lesson, theory, article, poetry
เพลง	song

Using wrong classification nouns is not really a serious matter as there is nothing to do with politeness at all but you can be sure that the Thai will laugh because it is just funny. Do not be discouraged when they laugh as they do not **laugh at** you. Your effort to try to speak their language has already won the Thai's appreciation.

สมุหนาม

is a group of prefixes which are put in front of nouns, adjectives, adverbs or verbs to make them to be noun. For example:

คน คนครัว (cook), คนสวน (gardener), คนใช้ (servant), คนขายของ (seller), คนซื้อ (buyer), คนไทย (Thai people)

ชาว ชาวอังกฤษ (British people), ชาวบ้าน (villager), ชาวนา (farmer)

ผู้	ผู้พูด (speaker), ผู้ฟัง (listener), ผู้ช่วย (assistant), ผู้ชาย (man), ผู้หญิง (woman), ผู้ใหญ่ (adult), ผู้เรียน (learner)	
ช่าง	ช่างไม้ (carpenter), ช่างตัดผม (hair dresser), ช่างตัดเสื้อ (dress maker), ช่างเครื่อง (mechanic), ช่างไฟฟ้า (electrician)	
นัก	นักเรียน (pupil), นักศึกษา (student), นักเขียน (writer), นักท่องเที่ยว (tourist)	

You may try to invent your own compound words from those prefixes. There is a fair chance to do it correctly. When it is wrong, like with classification nouns, it is not a really serious case.

Vocabulary:

ก.	ต้อง	-	must
ก.	กลัว	-	have fear
น.	ความมืด	-	darkness
ก.	เกลียด	-	hate
น.	เดิม	-	the same
น.	ร้านขายขนมปัง	-	bakery
น.	โรงภาพยนตร์	-	cinema
น.	อาคาร,ตึก	-	building
น.	ตา,ดวงตา	-	eyes
น.	บ้านเกิด(เมืองนอน)	-	home, motherland
ค.	ที่รัก	-	dear
ว.	ยิ่ง	-	very
น.	ความรัก	-	love
น.	มีด	-	knife

Lesson IX

ประโยค (Sentence) และ ก็

Forming a sentence in Thai language is fairly easy because words do not change their forms. The most important thing is the word order which dominates the function and meaning of the sentence. There are 3 basic types of sentences that we will consider in this lesson.

❶ **Single sentence:** Its structure is subject + verb + ... This kind of sentence presents only one content. It has one subject and one verb.

without object:	เขาเดิน	He walks.
with object:	คนไทยกินข้าว	The Thai eat rice.

You can see that the subject stands at the first position, the second is the verb. If there is an object, it must follow the verb.

with object and adverb:	ฉันซื้อรถเมื่อวานนี้	I bought a car yesterday.
or	เมื่อวานนี้ฉันซื้อรถ	Yesterday I bought a car.

The adverb can stand at the beginning or at the end of the sentence but it can never stand between the subject and verb or between verb and object.

Remark: The sentence with มี (there is, there are ...) is also regarded as a single sentence. For example

มีคนมากในตลาด   There are many people in the market.

❷ **Combined sentence:** Its structure is single sentence + conjunction + single sentence + ... This kind of sentences comprises of single sentences which are linked together by conjunction(s).

A) The single sentences have the same direction of meanings or support each other. For example:

	เขาออกกำลังกาย	He did body exercise.
	เขาอาบน้ำ	He had shower.
=	เขาออกกำลังกาย**แล้วจึง**อาบน้ำ	He did body exercise **then** had shower.
or	**หลังจาก**ออกกำลังกาย**แล้ว** เขา**จึง**อาบน้ำ	**After** having done body exercise, he had shower.
	เขาฟังมาก	He listens much.
	เขาอ่านมาก	He reads much.
	เขาเขียนมาก	He writes much.
=	เขาฟังมาก อ่านมาก**และ**เขียนมาก	He listens, reads, **and** writes much.
	เขาไปทำงาน	He went to work.
	ฉันไปโรงเรียน	I went to school.
=	**พอ**เขาไปทำงาน(แล้ว) ฉันก็ไปโรงเรียน	**After** he had (already) gone to work, I went to school.

B) The single sentences have different directions of meanings, e.g.

	พ่อฉลาด	The father is intelligent.
	ลูกโง่	The child is stupid.
=	พ่อฉลาด**แต่**ลูกโง่	The father is intelligent **but** the child is stupid.

	เขาตัวโต	He is big.
	ผมไม่กลัว	I am not afraid.
=	ถึงเขา(จะ)ตัวโต(แต่)ผมก็ไม่กลัว	Although he is big, I am not afraid.
	เรายากจน	We are poor.
	เรามีความสุข	We are happy.
=	แม้(ว่า)เรา(จะ)ยากจน (แต่)เราก็มีความสุข	Although we are poor, we are happy.

C) The single sentences have different directions of meanings between which one must choose:

	คุณจะไปประเทศไทย	You will go to Thailand.
	คุณจะไปประเทศญี่ปุ่น	You will go to Japan.
=	คุณจะไปประเทศไทย**หรือ**ประเทศญี่ปุ่น	Will you go to Thailand **or** Japan?
	เธอไม่ชอบข้าว	You do not like rice.
	เธอกินขนมปัง	You eat bread.
=	**ถ้า**เธอไม่ชอบข้าว **ก็**กินขนมปังซิ	**If** you don't like rice, just eat bread.
	ผู้ชายคนนี้บ้า	This man is mad.
	ผู้ชายคนนี้เมา	This man is drunken.
=	**หาก**ผู้ชายคนนี้ไม่บ้า เขา**ก็**ต้องเมา	**If** this man is not mad, he must be drunken.

D) One single sentence is the reason of the other, e.g.

	เขาทำความผิด	He is guilty.
	เขาติดคุก	He is put in prison.
=	เขาทำความผิด**เลย**ติดคุก	He is guilty, **so** he is put in prison.
	เขาทำงานหนัก	He works hard.
	เขารวย	He is rich.
=	เขาทำงานหนัก(**ดังนั้น**)เขาจึงรวย	He works hard, **so** he is rich.
or	เขาทำงานหนัก(**เพราะฉะนั้น**) เขาจึงรวย	

Remark:

ดังนั้น or เพราะฉะนั้น are actually not really needed, especially in spoken language. Only จึง is sufficient. All single sentences in a combined sentence are **main clause**.

❸ **Relative sentence:** Its structure is main clause + subordinate clause. Both clauses are linked by a relative pronoun, e.g.

Main clause:	ครูใจดี	The teacher is kind.
Subord. clause:	ครูสอนภาษาไทย	She teaches Thai.
=	ครู**ซึ่ง**สอนภาษาไทยใจดี	The teacher, **who** teaches Thai, is kind.

Main clause:	บ้านไม่จำเป็นต้องใหญ่โต	The house does not need to be big.
Subord. clause:	บ้านอบอุ่น	The house is cosy.
=	บ้าน**อัน**อบอุ่นไม่จำเป็นต้องใหญ่โต	The house, **which** is cosy, does not need to be big.

Main clause:	ฉันรักฤดูใบไม้ผลิ	I love spring.
Subord. clause:	ฤดูใบไม้ผลิมีดอกไม้สวยมากมาย	Spring has so many beautiful flowers.
=	ฉันรักฤดูใบไม้ผลิ**ที่**มีดอกไม้สวยมากมาย	I love spring, **which** has so many beautiful flowers.

Remark: The most often used relative pronouns are ที่,ซึ่ง,อัน

แบบฝึกหัดไวยากรณ์ (Grammar exercise)

Please fill in the following sentences with the provided alternatives:

หรือ,เพราะ,ก็,ซึ่ง,กำลัง,จึง,แต่,มี,ก็

1. เขากินจุ นอนมาก............ทำงานน้อย
2. เขาสูบบุหรี่จัด...........เป็นมะเร็งปอด
3. ขณะที่ผมทำงาน น้อง..........นอน
4. พอพ่อไปทำงานแล้ว แม่.........เริ่มทำงานบ้าน
5. ....การแข่งขันฟุตบอลที่กรุงเทพฯวันนี้
6. เขารักเธอ...........เธอสวย
7. ถ้าเขาไม่เรียน............โง่
8. คุณจะอยู่ในประเทศสหรัฐอเมริกา..........จะกลับไปประเทศไทย
9. เราเรียนภาษาไทย..........ง่ายและสนุก

How to use ก็

You have seen ก็ several times especially in this lesson. Let's study how to use this word more in detail. ก็ can mean many things:

❶ พอ.......ก็ is a conjunction for a combined sentence (point A), e.g.

พอคุณเรียก เราก็มาทันที   As soon as you call us, we come at once.

❷ ถึง......ก็,แม้......ก็ are conjunctions for a combined sentence (point B). It means **although**.

❸ ถ้า....ก็ is a conjunction for a combined sentence (point C). It mean**s if**.

❹ ก็เลย is a conjunction for a combined sentence (point D). It is more often used in spoken language and has the meaning of **so**, such as

การสอบใกล้เข้ามา นักเรียน   The examination is coming near, **so**
ก็เลยต้องขยัน   the students must be hard working.

❺ The answer **ก็ได้** means "yes" but it shows that the speaker is not very willing or eager to say it. Another possibility of this kind of answer is verb + **ก็** + verb. For example:

ไปดูหนังด้วยกันไหม   Will you go to the cinema with (me)?

(ไป)ก็ได้ or **ไปก็ไป**   O.K.

❻ ก็ดี can be used for the answer "That's not bad" or "I agree" or "It's O.K." The tone of ก็ดี also shows that the speaker is not very eager to say this or he is not much interested but it is anyway acceptable. For example:

อาหารร้านนี้อร่อยมากนะ   The food in this restaurant is very
   delicious, isn't it?
ก็ดี   It's **all right**.

❼ Noun or pronoun + **ก็ดี** ... For example:

เสื้อก็ดี กางเกงก็ดี ต้องสะอาด   Shirts, trousers must be clean.

In this case **ก็ดี** does not have any real meaning. It is only put behind a noun in order to make the sentence softer.

❽ ก็ shows consequences and has the sense of **also**. For example:

ผมชอบอาหารไทย คุณล่ะ	I like Thai food, and you?
ผมก็ชอบ(เหมือนกัน)	So do I.

Vocabulary:

ก.	ออกกำลังกาย	-	to do body exercise
สัน.	หลังจาก	-	after
ก.,ค.	ตัวโต	-	have big body
น.	ขนมปัง	-	bread
ค.,ว.	บ้า	-	mad
ค.	เมา	-	drunken
น.	ความผิด	-	guilt
ก.	ติด	-	stick, dependent on, addicted to
น.	คุก	-	prison
ก.	ติดคุก	-	be put in prison
ค.,ว.	หนัก	-	heavy, hard
ค.	รวย	-	rich
ก.	จำเป็น	-	need
น.	ฤดูใบไม้ผลิ	-	spring
ว.	(กิน)จุ	-	(eat) much
ว.	(สูบบุหรี่)จัด	-	(smoke) much
น.	มะเร็งปอด	-	lung cancer
สัน.	ขณะที่	-	while
ก.	เริ่ม	-	begin
น.	การแข่งขันฟุตบอล	-	soccer match
ว.	กลับ	-	back, go back

ว.	ทันที	-	at once, immediately
น.	การสอบ	-	examination
น.	หนัง, ภาพยนต์	-	film, movie
ว.	ด้วยกัน	-	together
น.	ร้านอาหาร, ภัตตาคาร	-	restaurant
น.	กางเกง	-	trousers

☑ Grammar exercise

1. แต่   2. จึง   3. กำลัง   4. ก็   5. มี
6. เพราะ   7. ก็   8. หรือ   9. ซึ่ง

Lesson X

คำถามและคำตอบ
(Questions and Answers)

There are 2 different types of questions. One can ask by using question words like ใคร, อะไร etc. or by putting expressions like ใช่ไหม etc. at the end of the sentence.

Question words:

❶ อะไร (what):

- When อะไร is a subject, its position is at the beginning of the sentence.

อะไรอร่อย	**What** tastes good?
อาหารทะเล	Sea food.

- When อะไร is an object, its position is at the end of the sentence.

คุณต้องการ**อะไร**	**What** do you want?
เงิน	Money.

Noun + อะไร or **Noun + แบบไหน** = what kind of ...:

คุณชอบอ่านหนังสือ**อะไร**	**What kind of** book do you like to read?
นิยาย	Novel.
คุณชอบดูหนัง**แบบไหน**	**What kind of** film do you like to watch?
หนังตลก	Comedy.

Useful phrases

(คุณ)เป็นอะไรไป	What happened (with you)?
เกิดอะไรขึ้น	What happened?

❷ ใคร (who, whom)

- ใคร as "who" is positioned at the beginning of a sentence.

ใครคือมาเทียส	Who is Matthias?
สามีของดิฉันค่ะ	My husband.

Exception:

คุณเป็นใคร	Who are you?
ผมเป็นตำรวจ	I am police officer.
ผมคือพ่อของนุชครับ	I am the father of Nut.
ดิฉันชื่อทิพย์วรรณ อาโบลด์ค่ะ	My name is Tipawan Abold.

- ใคร as "whom" is positioned at the end of a sentence.

คุณรักใคร	Whom do you love?
คุณ	You.
เขาให้ดอกไม้(แก่)ใคร	Whom did he give flowers?
สุนี	Suni.

❸ ...ของใคร (whose): The position can be both at the beginning or at the end of a sentence, e.g.

ลูกสาวของใครสวย	Whose daughter is beautiful?
ของผมครับ	Mine.

❹ อย่างไร, ยังไง (how): is always at the end of a sentence.

เราจะไปสถานีรถไฟได้อย่างไร	How can we get to the railway station?

ขึ้นรถรางสาย 2	With the tram No. 2.

Remark: ยังไง is only used in spoken language.

❺ เมื่อไร (when) และ กี่โมง (at what time): These words can be positioned both at the beginning and at the end of a sentence.

Remark: กี่โมง is only used when asking about the time.

เมื่อไรคุณจะมาเมืองไทยอีก	**When** will you come to Thailand again?
ปีหน้าครับ	Next year.
เครื่องบินออก**เมื่อไร**	**When** does the plane depart?
หกโมงยี่สิบ	18.20.
คุณตื่นนอน**กี่โมง**	**At what** time do you get up?
เจ็ดโมงครับ	7.00.
ขอโทษครับ **กี่โมง**แล้วครับ	Excuse me, please. **What** time is it?
แปดโมงครึ่งค่ะ	8.30.

❻ ที่ไหน, ไหน (where): This word can only be positioned at the end of a sentence. Sometimes a preposition before ที่ไหน or ไหน is needed.

ร้านอาหารอยู่**ที่ไหน**	**Where** is the restaurant?
ที่ถนนสุขุมวิท ซอย 63	Sukumwit street, lane 63.
คุณมา<u>จาก</u>**ไหน**	**Where** do you come <u>from</u>?
(<u>จาก</u>)กรุงเทพฯค่ะ	(From) Bangkok.
รถประจำทางคันนี้ไป**ไหน**คะ	**Where** does this bus go?
ไปสถานีขนส่งสายใต้ครับ	To the southern bus terminal.

❼ ทำไม (why): It can be positioned both at the beginning and at the end of a sentence but the former sounds better.

ทำไมคุณไม่ชอบเขาคะ	**Why** don't you like him?
เพราะว่าเขาใจแคบครับ	**Because** he is narrow-minded.

⑧ ...**ไหน** (which):

When you want to use ไหน, you always have to have a classifier in front of it. The position of a classifier combined with ไหน is usually at the end of a sentence.

คุณต้องการเสื้อ<u>ตัว</u>**ไหน**คะ	**Which** blouse do you want?
<u>ตัว</u>สีขาวค่ะ	<u>The</u> white one.

⑨ **เท่าไร** (how much), **กี่** + classifier (how many): These two question words are positioned at the end of a sentence.

เสื้อตัวนี้ราคา**เท่าไร**ครับ	**How much** does this shirt cost?
400 บาทค่ะ	400 Baht.
คุณต้องการกางเกง**กี่**<u>ตัว</u>คะ	**How many** trousers do you want?
ตัวเดียวครับ	One only.

There is another kind of questions which one has to answer with ใช่,ค่ะ,ครับ (yes), ไม่ใช่ (no), ยัง (not yet), ไม่เลย (not at all), ไม่เท่าไร (not really), แล้ว (already), etc. These questions have a tag at the end of the sentence. For example:

① **ไหม**

คุณหิว**ไหม**คะ	Are you hungry?
หิวครับ	Yes.
ไม่(หิว)ครับ	No.
ไม่(หิว)เลยครับ	Not at all.

② **หรือ**

คุณสบายดี**หรือ**คะ	How are you? / Are you o.K?
ครับ ผมสบายดี	Yes, I am fine.
ไม่ค่อยสบายเท่าไรครับ	Not very well.

In order to answer the questions with ไหม or หรือ, you only need to repeat the verb if you want to answer with "Yes". For a "No"-answer, just use the negation word ไม่ either with or without the verb.

③ **ใช่ไหม** (correct? right?)

คุณเป็นชาวอเมริกัน **ใช่ไหม**คะ	You are American, **right?**
ใช่ครับ	Yes.
ไม่ใช่ครับ	No.

For a "Yes"-answer, just use ใช่ and for a "No"-answer, use ไม่ใช่.

④ **หรือเปล่า** (or not)

คุณจะไปด้วย**หรือเปล่า**คะ	Will you come along **or not?**
ไป(ด้วย)ครับ	Yes.
เปล่าค่ะ	No.

For a "Yes"-answer, just repeat the verb, for a "No"-answer, use the negation word เปล่า without the verb.

⑤ **(แล้ว)หรือยัง** (already or not yet)

คุณรับประทานอาหาร **แล้วหรือยัง**	Have you **already** eaten?

| แล้วค่ะ | Yes, already. |
| ยังค่ะ | No, not yet. |

For a "Yes"-answer, just use แล้ว or the verb + แล้ว. For a "No"-answer, use ยัง without the verb.

Vocabulary:

น.	อาหารทะเล	-	seafood
น.	หนังสือ	-	book
น.	หนังตลก	-	comedy
น.	ตำรวจ	-	police
น.	สถานีรถไฟ	-	railway station
ก.	ขึ้น(รถ)	-	to get in
น.	รถราง	-	tram
น.	ปีหน้า	-	next year
น.	เครื่องบิน	-	plane, aircraft
ก.	ออก	-	to depart
ก.	ตื่นนอน	-	wake up, get up
น.	รถประจำทาง	-	bus
น.	สถานีขนส่ง(สายใต้)	-	(southern) bus terminal
ก.,น.	ราคา	-	price, cost
ก.	ไปด้วย	-	to come along
ก.	รับประทาน,ทาน	-	eat, formal and very polite word for กิน

Lesson XI

คำสั่ง (Imperative) การปฏิเสธ (Negation) กรรมวาจก (Passive)

คำสั่ง (Imperative)

Basically an imperative is a simple sentence without subject. For example:

ไปนอน	Go to bed.
ทำการบ้าน	Do homework.

But the Thai have an art in softening their command by adding some particles at the end of an imperative. For example:

วิ่งเร็วๆเข้า	Run quickly.
ตื่นเถอะ	Wake up.
กินซิ	Eat.

Those particles are ซิ, เสีย, นะ, เถอะ, เถิด, ที, หน่อย, เสียที, เข้า. They make an order sound more like an advice, especially when you use a soft tone of voice. โปรด or กรุณา can be put in front of the sentence to make it even more polite or sound more like a request.

Please note that the Thai who may look gentle, friendly, humble or even passive are not fond of getting commands at all. They may not show any dissatisfaction but they really do not like it and they have their way to demonstrate their negative attitude against you which is sometimes not easy for foreigners to see or to feel but this can really cause problems in the long run. So if you have to work with the Thai, you should better use more requests or advices although you may think that you have the right to order them.

Sharp commands are however available in Thai language but they are more often used in written language. This kind of sentences can be easily made by adding จง in front of an imperative, e.g.

จงตอบคำถามต่อไปนี้	Answer the following questions.
จงเขียนเรียงความเรื่องอาหารไทย	Write a composition about Thai food.

Another kind of order is **negative command**. อย่า or ห้าม is needed in this case. Both can be used in written and spoken language but there is a small difference between them.

อย่า is more often used in conversation as it has a relatively softer tone than ห้าม which gives a very strict and sharp sense. Both words stand at the beginning of an imperative. For example:

อย่านอนดึก	**Don't** go to bed late.
ห้ามสูบบุหรี่	Smoking is **forbidden**.

การปฏิเสธ (Negation)

The word "not" is ไม่ in Thai language.

❶ ไม่ stands between **subject** and **verb**, e.g.

คนไทย**ไม่**ชอบเนยแข็ง	The Thai **do not** like cheese.
นักเรียน**ไม่**ทำการบ้าน	Pupils **do not** do homework.

❷ ไม่ stands between **helping verb** and **main verb** (except ต้อง, ควร, สามารถ). In this case we have to keep in mind that helping verbs in Thai can be different from those in English. Some Thai helping verbs are adverbs in your language such as ยังไม่ (not yet), คง (probably), อาจ, อาจจะ (perhaps).

พ่อยัง**ไม่**กลับบ้าน	Father does **not** come home **yet**.
เขา**คงไม่**เชื่อคุณ	She **probably doesn't** believe you.
เขา**จะไม่**ดื่มเบียร์	He **will not** drink beer.

❸ There are 2 possibilities in using ไม่ with ต้อง (must, have to):

- Subject + **ต้อง** + **ไม่** + main verb

  เขา**ต้องไม่**กินอาหารเผ็ด He **must not** eat spicy hot food.

- Subject + **ไม่** + **ต้อง** + main verb

  เขา**ไม่ต้อง**กินอาหารเผ็ด He **does not have to** eat spicy hot food.

❹ ไม่ stands between **subject** and the helping verbs **ควร** and **สามารถ** (read: สา + มาด).

| คุณ**ไม่ควร**ขับรถโดยประมาท | You **should not** drive carelessly. |
| ฉัน**ไม่สามารถ**ดื่มแอลกอฮอล์**ได้** | I **can not** drink alcohol. |

Remark:

ได้ is adverb which is normally used alone or together with the helping verb **สามารถ**. **ได้** stands at the end of the sentence and has the meaning of **can**.

❺ ไม่ stands in front of **adverb**. In this case, again, we have to study the difference between Thai and English grammars. There are a few **adverbs** in Thai which mean "can" in your language. They are ...ออก, ...เป็น, ...ได้. For example:

| เขาอ่านหนังสือ**ไม่ออก** | He **can't** read. (he is illiterate.) |
| ฉันว่ายน้ำ**ไม่เป็น** | I **can't** swim. (I don't know how to swim.) |

| ผมบอกคุณไม่ได้ | I can't tell you. (It is a secret.) |
| ผมทำไม่ได้ | I can't do it. |

The adverb ...**ออก** as "can" is used in the following idioms: คิดไม่ออก (can't figure it out), พูดไม่ออก (can't say it out because of some reasons), ดูไม่ออก (can't distinguish the value of something, can't understand someone or a situation), ฟังไม่ออก (you hear something but you don't understand it), etc.

The adverb ...**เป็น** as "can" shows capability or skill. We use this word with the ability or skill which one gets from learning or practising such as speaking a foreign language, cooking, playing music instruments, etc.

The adverb ...**ได้** as "can" is more often used in spoken language while the verb **สามารถ** (also means "can") is more common in writing. A sentence with **สามารถ** has, however, almost always **ได้** in addition at the end of the sentence. For example:

เขา**ไม่สามารถ**พูดภาษาเยอรมัน**ได้** = เขาพูดภาษาเยอรมัน**ไม่ได้**

By the way, there are some funny sentences in which you can not use the adverb ได้ as "can" at all. They are idioms which do not follow the rule. For example:

| I can't see it. | ผมมองไม่เห็น (not ผมเห็นไม่ได้) |
| I can't find it. | ผมหาไม่เจอ หรือ ผมหาไม่พบ (not ผมหาไม่ได้) |

More examples for the rule of ไม่ in a sentence with adverb.

| เขาเรียน**ไม่เก่ง** | He **does not** learn **well**. |
| สุดายิ้ม**ไม่สวย** | Suda **does not** smile **beautifully**. |

⑥ As you should have known by now that to form a sentence in the past, you do not need to do anything with the verb at all when it is clear that you are talking about the past, such as:

แม่ไปตลาด (เมื่อวานนี้)　　　　Mother **went** to the market (yesterday).

But if you want, you can also put ได้ in front of the verb to indicate past tense such as:

แม่ได้ไปตลาด　　　　Mother **went** to the market.

ได้ is here an adverb too but it does not mean "can" like in the rules 4 and 5. We can say that indicating past tense by using ได้ in an affirmative sentence is not needed at all **but** in a negative sentence ได้ is definitely needed because ไม่ must stand between the subject and ได้.

แม่**ไม่ได้**ไปตลาด (เมื่อวานนี้)　　　Mother **did not** go to the market (yesterday).

เมื่อปีก่อน ผม**ไม่ได้**ทำงานที่นี่　　　Last year I **did not** work here.

กรรมวาจก (Passive voice)

Passive voice is not often used in Thai and it is mainly used when one talks about an unpleasant event. There are 3 forms of Passive voice in Thai language.

❶ Active:　　Subject + Verb + Object
　　Passive:　　Object + ถูก + Subject + Verb

A	แม่ทำโทษนุช	Mother punishes Nud.
P	นุชถูกแม่ทำโทษ	Nud **is** punished by mother.
A	จอห์นฆ่าเพเทอร์	John killed Peter.
P	เพเทอร์ถูกจอห์นฆ่า	Peter **was** killed by John.

This form is normally used for a **very** unpleasant event and the objects are **mostly** human beings or at least animals. When you do not want to mention the doer, you can simply leave the subject out, such as นุชถูกทำโทษ หรือ เพเทอร์ถูกฆ่า

❷ Active: Subject + Verb + Object + ADVERB
   Passive: Object + ADVERB

A	ผมใช้เงิน**หมด**	I ran out of money.
P	เงิน**หมด**	Money was run out.
A	ป้าทำแก้ว**แตก**	Aunt broke a glass.
P	แก้ว**แตก**	A glass was broken.

In this case, things are not so bad as in ❶ although they are not nice either. **Mostly** the objects are things.

❸ Active: Subject + Verb + Object
   Passive: Object + Verb + **โดย** + Subject

A	บิลเขียนจดหมายฉบับนี้	Bill wrote this letter.
P	จดหมายฉบับนี้เขียน**โดย**บิล	This letter was written **by** Bill.

This form obviously got influence from passive voice in English and it is very rarely used. **Mostly** the objects are things and the events are not unpleasant.

Vocabulary:

น.	เรียงความ	-	composition
ค.	เผ็ด	-	spicy hot
ว.	โดยประมาท	-	carelessly
น.	ภาษาเยอรมัน	-	German language

ก.	ทำโทษ	-	punish
ก.	ฆ่า, ฆาตกรรม	-	kill
ก., ค., ว.	หมด	-	empty, run out of
ค., ก.	ทำแตก	-	break
น.	จดหมาย	-	letter

Lesson XII

การนับ เวลา และวันที่
Counting, Time and Date

การนับและตัวเลข (counting and figures)

0	ศูนย์	1	หนึ่ง	2	สอง
3	สาม	4	สี่	5	ห้า
6	หก	7	เจ็ด	8	แปด
9	เก้า	10	สิบ	11	สิบเอ็ด
12	สิบสอง	13	สิบสาม	14	สิบสี่
15	สิบห้า	16	สิบหก	17	สิบเจ็ด
18	สิบแปด	19	สิบเก้า	20	ยี่สิบ
21	ยี่สิบเอ็ด	22	ยี่สิบสอง	23	ยี่สิบสาม
30	สามสิบ	31	สามสิบเอ็ด	32	สามสิบสอง
40	สี่สิบ	50	ห้าสิบ	60	หกสิบ
100	(หนึ่ง)ร้อย	101	(หนึ่ง)ร้อยเอ็ด	102	(หนึ่ง)ร้อยสอง
200	สองร้อย	201	สองร้อยเอ็ด	202	สองร้อยสอง
1,000	(หนึ่ง)พัน	1,100	(หนึ่ง)พันหนึ่งร้อย		
10,000	(หนึ่ง)หมื่น	11,000	(หนึ่ง)หมื่นหนึ่งพัน		
100,000	(หนึ่ง)แสน	110,000	(หนึ่ง)แสนหนึ่งหมื่น		
1,000,000	(หนึ่ง)ล้าน	1,100,000	(หนึ่ง)ล้านหนึ่งแสน		

ตัวเลขไทย (Thai figures)

๐ ๑ ๒ ๓ ๔ ๕ ๖ ๗ ๘ ๙ ๑๐...

These figures are no more very often used.

ลำดับที่ (Sequence)

1. ที่หนึ่ง   2. ที่สอง   3. ที่สาม   11. ที่สิบเอ็ด..........

เวลา (Time)

The official time system is relatively easy to learn, as it uses the 24-hours time. Just put the word นาฬิกา (o'clock) at the end of each hour.

08.00 a.m.	แปดนาฬิกา
08.15 a.m.	แปดนาฬิกาสิบห้านาที
08.30 a.m.	แปดนาฬิกาสามสิบนาที
08.00 p.m.	ยี่สิบนาฬิกา

The traditional time system which is more often used is a bit more complicated. It uses a 6 hours (ชั่วโมง) circle.

เที่ยงคืน	midnight		ตีหนึ่ง	01.00 a.m.
ตีสอง	02.00 a.m.		ตีสาม	03.00 a.m.
ตีสี่	04.00 a.m.		ตีห้า	05.00 a.m.
หกโมง(เช้า)	06.00 a.m.		เจ็ดโมง(เช้า)	07.00 a.m.
		or	(หนึ่ง)โมงเช้า	07.00 a.m.
แปดโมง(เช้า)	08.00 a.m.		เก้าโมง(เช้า)	09.00 a.m.
or สองโมง(เช้า)	08.00 a.m.	or	สามโมง(เช้า)	09.00 a.m.
สิบโมง(เช้า)	10.00 a.m.		สิบเอ็ดโมง	11.00 a.m.
or สี่โมง(เช้า)	10.00 a.m.	or	ห้าโมง(เช้า)	11.00 a.m.

เที่ยง(วัน)	midday	บ่ายโมง	01.00 p.m.
(บ่าย)สองโมง	02.00 p.m.	(บ่าย)สามโมง	03.00 p.m.
or สองโมงเย็น	02.00 p.m.	or สามโมงเย็น	03.00 p.m.
สี่โมงเย็น	04.00 p.m.	ห้าโมงเย็น	05.00 p.m.
หกโมงเย็น	06.00 p.m.	หนึ่งทุ่ม	07.00 p.m.
สองทุ่ม	08.00 p.m.	สามทุ่ม	09.00 p.m.
สี่ทุ่ม	10.00 p.m.	ห้าทุ่ม	11.00 p.m.
ห้าทุ่ม**ตรง**	11.00 p.m. sharp	ห้าทุ่ม**กว่า**	shortly after 11.00 p.m.
เกือบห้าทุ่ม	almost 11.00 p.m.	นาฬิกา	watch, clock, o'clock
ชั่วโมง	hour	นาที	minute
วินาที	second	ครึ่งชั่วโมง	half an hour
ตอนเช้า	in the morning	ตอนสาย	late morning
ตอนกลางวัน	during the day	ตอนบ่าย	afternoon
ตอนเย็น	late afternoon	ตอนค่ำ	evening
ตอนกลางคืน	at night	ก่อน	before
หลัง	after	ระหว่าง	between
เมื่อไรก็ได้	anytime	เสมอ, ทุกที	always
นาน	long	บ่อย	often
ไม่เคย	never	ในไม่ช้า, เร็วๆนี้	soon
บางที, บางครั้ง	sometimes	สาย, ดึก	late

วันที่ (Date)

The Thai count the dates in the same way as the numbers. Just put the word วันที่ in front of a number, for example:

วันที่หนึ่ง	1.	วันที่สอง	2.
วันที่สาม	3.	วันที่สิบ	10.
วันที่สิบเอ็ด	11.	วันที่ยี่สิบ	20.
วันนี้	today	พรุ่งนี้	tomorrow
มะรืนนี้	the day after tomorrow	(เมื่อ)วานนี้	yesterday
เมื่อวานซืน	the day before yesterday	วันก่อน	a day which already passed
วันหน้า	a day in the future	วันหลัง	a day which will come later

Lesson XIII

Some more grammar rules

❶ หลักการเขียน ใ- หรือ ไ- (Rules of ใ- or ไ-)

There are actually only 20 **basic** words which use ใ-. They are:

ใหญ่ (big)

ใหม่ (new)

ให้ (give, let ...)

สะใภ้ (in law)

ใช้ (use, spend, utilize, exploit, ...)

ใฝ่ (to pay attention, to have an interest in ....)

ใจ (heart, mind, feeling)

ใส่ (to wear, to put, with ...)

ใคร (who, whom, people, someone)

ใคร่ (want, desire)

หลงใหล (passion, adore)

ใบ (leaf, sheet, ticket, blade, licence)

ใส (clear, bright)

ใด (which)

ใน (in)

ใช่ (yes, correct, exact)

ใต้ (south, under)

ใบ้ (dumb)

ใย (fibre, thread)

ใกล้ (near)

The problem is that these 20 words can be combined with others to become new compound words such as คนใช้ (servant), แจ่มใส (bright), น้ำใจ (sympathy, kindness), สายใย (net, line), etc. So you have to consider the meaning of the compound words which the context can help much. In fact it is not too difficult because you can always see that the meanings of the new words have something to do with the meaning of those basic words, such as any word with ใจ always concerns with heart, feeling, mind, or emotion.

Apart from words which derive from these 20 words with ใ-, we use ไ-, such as ไหม (silk, question tag), ไจ (hank of yarn), ไส (push, drive away), ตะไคร่ (moss), ไหล (to flow, to run), etc.

❷ หลักการอ่าน ฤ (Rules of ฤ)

When ฤ is in words, ฤ can be pronounced in 3 ways:

① ฤ is pronounced ริ when ฤ is vowel of ก, ต, ท, ป, ศ, ส, e.g. ฤทธิ์ (magical power) is read ริด. ทฤษฎี (theory) is read ทริด + สะ + ดี.

② ฤ is pronounced รึ when ฤ is vowel of ค, น, พ, ม, ห, e.g. พฤษภาคม (May) is read พรึด + สะ + พา + คม or when ฤ stands as the first syllable of the word, such as ฤดู (season) is read รึ + ดู.

③ ฤ is pronounced เรอ. This case has only one word which is ฤกษ์ (auspicious occasion or time). ฤกษ์ is read เริก.

❸ The complicated เป็น, มี, มา, ไป, เพื่อ, เล่น, ถือ, ได้, พอ

160

① **เป็น:** Verb to be is normally translated เป็น, อยู่ or คือ. They are however not really the same.

อยู่ has the sense of remain, stay, life,...: e.g.

เขาอยู่บ้าน	He **stays** home.
เขาอยู่บ้านนี้	He **lives** in this house.
เขายังมีชีวิตอยู่	He **is** still **alive**.

คือ is very often used in the same way as เป็น but คือ has more introductory sense and sounds more formal: e.g.

เขา**เป็น**พ่อของผม = He **is** my father. = เขา **คือ**พ่อของผม

In some cases, เป็น as verb to be can not be replaced by คือ at all, especially when the word which follows เป็น is an adjective, such as ผม**เป็น**สุขมาก (I am very happy).

Let's say the words before and after **คือ must refer to the same person or thing**, e.g. **เขาคือพ่อของผม**: เขาและพ่อ are the same person but ผมเป็นสุข: ผม = I, สุข = happy.

เป็น is widely used in many ways so it is much more complicated than the others.

เป็น is used exactly like verb to be in English in only a few cases, such as เป็นสุข (to be happy), เป็นทุกข์ (to be unhappy), เป็นโสด (to be single), เป็นบ้า (to be mad), เป็นกลาง (to be neutral).

เป็น can also be used to indicate status, occupation, relation, such as เป็นเด็ก (to be a child), เป็นครู (to be a teacher), เป็นแม่ (to be a mother), ... When verb to be in English is followed by an adjective, เป็น is in Thai left out, such as:

She **is beautiful**.	เขา**สวย**
He **is good**.	เขา**ดี**.

In this case, the adjective is in Thai regarded as the verb itself. So เป็น is no more needed.

About **illness**, when verb **to have** (มี) is used in English, verb to be (เป็น) may be needed in Thai or neither verb to have nor verb to be is needed at all, such as:

    I **have** cancer.   ผมเป็นมะเร็ง
    I **have** pain here.   ดิฉันเจ็บตรงนี้

เป็น has also the sense of "life" or "to live" in some cases, such as ปลาเป็น (alive fish), หน้าเป็น (the face which looks so lively because of always smiling or laughing), ความเป็นอยู่ (living, the way of life), เผาตายทั้งเป็น (burnt alive), etc.

② **มี** is normally **verb to have** in English but มี can also mean **there is** and **there are** when มี is used without subject, such as

มีไข่2ฟองในตะกร้า   **There are** 2 eggs in the basket.

Remark:
Apart from เป็นสุข, **to be happy** can be also translated **มีความสุข** in Thai, such us

เขาเป็นสุขมาก = เขามีความสุขมาก = He is very **happy**.

③ **มา and ไป:** Normally **มา** means **to come** and **ไป** means **to go** but in some cases, these 2 words are not used as **verb** but **preposition** or **adverb**. Yet they indicate movement, such as:

ผมขอโทรศัพท์**ไป**ออสเตรเลียครับ   I would like to telephone **to** Australia.
มีข่าว**มา**จากสหรัฐอเมริกา   There is news **from** U.S.A.
ลมพัดใบไม้ปลิว**ไป**   The wind blows leaves **away**.

When it is about time, มา and ไป have more complication, e.g.

คุณ**อยู่**เมืองไทยนานเท่าไร   How long did you **stay** in Thailand?

This sentence says that you don't stay in Thailand anymore, but

คุณ**อยู่**เมืองไทย**มา**นานเท่าไร(แล้ว) How long **have** you **lived** in Thailand?

This sentence says that you still live in Thailand. About the time, **มา** as adverb indicates present perfect tense.

เขา**ไป**กรุงเทพฯแล้ว   He **went** to Bangkok *or* He **has gone** to Bangkok.

This sentence says that he went to Bangkok and he has not come back yet but เขา**ไป**กรุงเทพฯ**มา** means He **has been** in Bangkok. (He **has already come** back.)

④ **เพื่อ** generally means "for" and it is a **preposition**.

เพื่อคุณ   For you.

เพื่อ as "**for**" sounds a little bit formal but it is a beautiful word, so it is more often used in written language. In spoken language, you can hear **สำหรับ** or **ให้** more often.

เขาทำอาหาร**ให้**คุณ   He cooks **for** you.

เสื้อตัวนี้**สำหรับ**คุณ   This blouse is **for** you.

เพื่อ can be also a **conjunction** and it means "in order to".

	เขาไปซื้อของที่ตลาด	She goes shopping in the market.
=	เขาไปตลาด**เพื่อ**ซื้อของ	
หรือ	เขาไปตลาด**เพื่อ**จะซื้อของ	→She goes to the market (**in order**)
หรือ	เขาไปตลาด**เพื่อที่จะ**ซื้อของ	to buy things.
หรือ	เขาไปตลาด**เพื่อ**ว่า(เขา)จะซื้อของ	She goes to the market **in order that** she will buy things.

⑤ **เล่น** means in general "to play".

In Thai sport and music are mainly combined with "to play" because the Thai regard them as entertainment. So the Thai use เล่น with almost all kinds of sports and music instruments.

Apart from เล่นกีฬา (to do sports) and เล่นดนตรี (to play music instruments), the Thai also เล่นการเมือง (to be politician). With politics the Thai also use เล่น. What does the phrase เล่นการเมือง reflect? Just look at the Thai politics!!!

The word เล่น is used with many other words to show that they are not a serious matter, such as ของเล่น (toy), นอนเล่น (just lie down to have a rest or because of having nothing to do, not to really sleep), เดินเล่น (to have a stroll), กินเล่น (to have snack or sweet just because one likes to have, not because of real hunger.), etc.

⑥ **ถือ** generally means "to hold or to have something in hand"

เขาถือกระเป๋าสีน้ำตาล	She **carries** a brown bag.

But ถือ can also mean "take something as a serious matter"

คนไทยถือว่าศีรษะเป็นของสูง	The Thai **regard** head as noble part (of the body).
อย่าใช้เท้าชี้สิ่งต่างๆ	Don't point at things with (your) foot.
คนไทยถือว่า นั่นไม่สุภาพ	The Thai **regard** it as impolite.

Remark:

The head is the most noble part of the body for the Thai. Therefore please do not touch their heads.

Please never point with the foot at someone or something. This is very bad manners for the Thai.

In case you are invited to the house of a Thai family, please put off your shoes before entering the house.

It is not very acceptable in Thai culture for a man to touch a woman unless they are a couple. Please try to avoid it if you are not sure that the woman understands the cultural difference between the east and the west.

⑦ **ได้** can mean many things.

- **ได้** indicates past tense.

เขา**ได้**พบฉันเมื่อวานนี้	He **met** me yesterday.

- **ได้** as adverb shows capability or skill.

เขาพูดไทย**ได้**	He **can** speak Thai.

- **ได้** as main verb means to get, to receive, to win, to profit.

ในคาสิโนเมื่อคืนนี้ เขา**ได้**มากกว่าเสีย	In the casino last night, he **won** more than lost.
ผม**ได้**จดหมายของคุณแล้ว	I have **got** your letter.

⑧ **พอ** in general means "enough". For example:

พอแล้ว	Enough.
เขามีเงินมาก**พอ**ที่จะซื้อบ้านหลังโต	He has money **enough** to buy a big house.

พอดี means just right, just good, e.g.

กางเกงตัวนี้คับไปไหม(สำหรับผม)	Are these trousers too small (for me)?
พอดีแล้ว	(It is) **just right** (for you).
ลองชิมแกงจืดหน่อยซิคะ เค็มเกินไปไหมคะ	Please try the soup. Is it too salted?

พอดีแล้วครับ   (It is) **just good.**

Vocabulary:

น.	ชีวิต	-	life
น.	มะเร็ง	-	cancer
น.	ตะกร้า	-	basket
น.	ลม	-	wind
น.	ใบไม้	-	leaf
น.	กีฬา	-	sport
น.	ดนตรี	-	music
น.	การเมือง	-	politics
น.	กระเป๋า	-	bag
น.	ศีรษะ (สี + สะ)	-	head (หัว means head too but ศีรษะ is more polite)
น.,ค.	ของสูง	-	noble
น.	เท้า	-	foot
ก.	ชี้	-	point at
น.	สิ่งต่างๆ	-	things
ค.,ว.	สุภาพ	-	polite
ค.	คับ	-	narrow, small
ก.	ลองชิม	-	try (the taste of food)

Lesson XIV

จดหมาย
Letter

The basic rules are: the content, style of writing, language, salutation and greetings must be suitable to the purpose of the letter, the status and age of the receiver and sender as well as the relationship between the 2 parties.

Private letter:

Receivers	Salutation	Greetings
very close, important, elder relatives: parents, grand parents	กราบเท้า...ที่เคารพอย่างสูง	ด้วยความเคารพอย่างสูง
close, important, elder relatives: uncles, aunts...	กราบ ... ที่เคารพ(อย่างสูง)	ด้วยความเคารพ(อย่างสูง)
elder brothers and sisters	พี่ ... ที่รัก พี่ ... ที่เคารพ	ด้วยความรัก ด้วยความเคารพ
friends, younger brothers or sisters	น้อง ... ที่รัก, ... ที่คิดถึง เพื่อน ... ที่รัก, ...ที่คิดถึง	ด้วยความรัก รักและคิดถึง
respected older people	กราบเรียน...ที่เคารพ(อย่างสูง) เรียน...ที่เคารพ(อย่างสูง)	ด้วยความเคารพ(อย่างสูง)
monks	นมัสการ	นมัสการมาด้วยความเคารพอย่างสูง

Example of an easy envelope label:

```
ผู้ส่ง
ทิพย์วรรณ  ธรรมผุสนา
564/9  หมู่  3   แขวงคลองขวาง
เขตภาษีเจริญ  กรุงเทพฯ  10160

กรุณาส่ง      คุณวัลลีย์  สว่างแวว
              เทศบาลตำบลหัวหิน
              458  ถนนเพชรเกษม
              อำเภอหัวหิน
              จังหวัดประจวบคีรีขันธ์  77110
```

Example of a private letter:

564/9 ม. 3 คลองขวาง ภาษีเจริญ
กรุงเทพฯ 10160

15 กรกฎาคม 2537

แตงน้องรัก

    ก่อนอื่น พี่ต้องขอโทษที่ตอบจดหมายช้ามาก ทั้งนี้เพราะระหว่างนี้พ่อของพี่ไม่ค่อยสบาย ต้องเข้าโรงพยาบาลถึง 2 อาทิตย์ ทางบ้านเราก็เลยวุ่นวายกันพอสมควร แม่ต้องไปเฝ้าใช้ งานในบริษัทก็ยุ่งและพี่ต้องทำงานบ้านทั้งหมดแทนแม่ รวมทั้งช่วยดูแลพ่อด้วย

    เรื่องที่แตงเล่ามานั้น พี่เข้าใจและรู้สึกเห็นใจแตงมาก แต่ก็อยากให้แตงใจเย็นๆไว้ก่อน ที่ว่าจะลาออกจากงานนั้น พี่ไม่เห็นด้วย เพราะสมัยนี้งานดีๆหายาก แตงเองก็รู้ พี่คิดว่าแตงควรจะให้เวลาคุณทวีอีกสักหน่อย แกเป็นเจ้านายที่ไม่เลว พี่เชื่อว่าแกจะพิจารณาแก้ไขปัญหาระหว่างแตงกับคุณสมหญิงด้วยความยุติธรรม

    ขอส่งกำลังใจให้น้องที่พี่รักยิ่ง ขอจงเข้มแข็ง เยือกเย็น และอดทน พี่แน่ใจว่าในไม่ช้าปัญหาทั้งปวงจะคลี่คลายไปในทางที่ดี

รักเสมอ
พี่

Vocabulary:

น.	ผู้ส่ง	-	sender
น.	ผู้รับ	-	receiver
น.	หมู่ , ม.	-	house group
น.	แขวง,ตำบล,ต.	-	sub region, comprising of some house groups
น.	เขต,อำเภอ,อ.	-	district, comprising of some sub regions
น.	เทศบาล	-	municipality administration
น.	จังหวัด,จ.	-	province
	2537		1994 (In Thailand the official year is Buddhist year, which started after the death of Buddha. The difference between the Thai and the western year counting is 543 years.)
น.	รหัสไปรษณีย์ (เช่น 10160)	-	postal code (comes after the name of the province)
ว.	ก่อนอื่น	-	at first
สัน.	ทั้งนี้เพราะว่า..	-	this is because ....
ว.	ระหว่างนี้	-	during this time
ก.	เข้าโรงพยาบาล	-	to be admitted in a hospital
ว.	ถึง,ตั้ง	-	adverb, usually followed by a number or an amount to show the opinion of the speaker that it is really much, for example ถึง 2 อาทิตย์ or ตั้ง 20 บาท
น.	ทางบ้านเรา	-	our family
ว.	พอสมควร	-	reasonably, fairly
ก.	เฝ้าไข้	-	take care of a patient. (As the family relation in Thailand is still very close, it is common that one stays with the ill family member in the hospital, when they can afford a private room, in order to take care and give the patient morale support.)

ว.	แทน	-	for
บ.	รวมทั้ง	-	including
ก.	ช่วย	-	help
ก.	ดูแล	-	take care
น.	เรื่อง	-	story, legend, issue, case
ก.	เล่า	-	tell
สัน.	ที่ว่า ...	-	That ...
ก.	ลาออก (จากงาน)	-	to quit (a job)
น.	สมัยนี้	-	nowadays
ก.	หา	-	find, search for
ค.,ว.	สักหน่อย	-	a bit
ก.	พิจารณา	-	consider
ก.	แก้ไข	-	solve
น.	ปัญหา	-	problem
บ.	ระหว่าง....กับ.....	-	between ... and ...
น.	ความยุติธรรม	-	fairness
น.	กำลังใจ	-	encouragement
ค.,ก.	เข้มแข็ง	-	strong
ค.,ก.	เยือกเย็น	-	calm
ก.	แน่ใจ	-	to be sure
ค.	ทั้งปวง	-	all
ก.	คลี่คลาย	-	develop, to be solved

Example of a business letter:

73/2 ถนนมนตรีสุริยวงศ์ อ.เมือง

ราชบุรี 70000

20 เมษายน 2537

เรื่อง   การเดินทางท่องเที่ยวในประเทศญี่ปุ่น
เรียน   ผู้อำนวยการบริษัทเถกิงทัวร์ จำกัด
อ้างถึง   จดหมายของบริษัทเถกิงทัวร์ จำกัด ฉบับลงวันที่ 31 มีนาคม 2537
สิ่งที่ส่งมาด้วย   1. หนังสือเดินทางเลขที่ T 089545
             2. รูปถ่ายขนาด 3 นิ้ว 2 รูป
             3. เช็คเงินสดมัดจำค่าเดินทาง 1 ฉบับ มูลค่า 1000 บาท

   ด้วยดิฉันได้รับข้อเสนอและกำหนดการเดินทางไปท่องเที่ยวที่ประเทศญี่ปุ่นจากบริษัทของท่านเมื่อสัปดาห์ที่แล้ว ดิฉันได้พิจารณาแล้วเห็นว่า รายการท่องเที่ยวของท่านน่าสนใจและมีความเหมาะสมทั้งในด้านสถานที่ท่องเที่ยว เวลาและค่าใช้จ่าย ดิฉันจึงใคร่ขอร่วมเดินทางไปประเทศญี่ปุ่นในครั้งนี้ด้วย

   พร้อมกับจดหมายฉบับนี้ ดิฉันได้ส่งรูปถ่าย หนังสือเดินทาง และเงินมัดจำค่าเดินทางมาให้ท่านด้วยแล้ว ดิฉันหวังว่าท่านจะรีบดำเนินการขอวีซ่าเข้าประเทศญี่ปุ่น และติดต่อกลับมายังดิฉันโดยเร็ว

ขอแสดงความนับถือ

(นางสาวรุจิรา สินสมุทร)

Vocabulary:

	เรื่อง ……….	-	re:
น.	การเดินทางท่องเที่ยว	-	journey
	เรียน ……….	-	Dear …
น.	ผู้อำนวยการ	-	director
	จำกัด	-	similar to a limited company
	อ้างถึง ……….	-	regarding
	สิ่งที่ส่งมาด้วย ……….	-	enclosure
น.	รูปถ่าย	-	passport picture
น.	ขนาด	-	size
น.	นิ้ว	-	inch
น.	เช็ค	-	cheque
น.	เงินสด	-	cash
น.,ก.	มัดจำ	-	instalment
น.	ค่าเดินทาง	-	travelling cost
น.	มูลค่า	-	value
สัน.,บ.	ด้วย	-	with, that
น.	ข้อเสนอ	-	offer
น.	กำหนดการ	-	schedule
น.	รายการ	-	program
ค.,ว.	น่าสนใจ	-	interesting
ก.	ความเหมาะสม	-	appropriation
น.	สถานที่ท่องเที่ยว	-	tourist attractions
น.	ค่าใช้จ่าย	-	expense
ก.	ใคร่	-	want
ก.	ร่วมเดินทาง	-	travel with
บ.	พร้อมกับ	-	together with, enclosed
ก.	หวัง	-	hope

ก.	รีบ	-	hurry
ก.	ดำเนินการ	-	carry out
ก.	ติดต่อ	-	contact
น.	นางสาว,น.ส.	-	Miss (single woman or girl above 15)
น.	เด็กหญิง,ด.ญ.	-	Miss (girl under 15 years)
น.	นาง	-	Mrs.
น.	เด็กชาย,ด.ช.	-	Mr. (boy under 15 years)
น.	นาย	-	Mr. (man or boy above 15 years)

ภาคผนวก
Appendix

In this part of the book you will find examples of conversation comprising different themes. The information given in each theme may be at a level helpful to you.

As you have already learned the basic Thai grammar from the first part of the book, you are now expected to be able to read, understand, and pronounce the dialogues yourself (in case you have difficulties, you should regard them as useful exercises!!!). Due to this reason you will not find the dialogues in the cassette. There is - on purpose - no vocabulary list included at the end of each theme either.

The themes of dialogues and their information:

❶ การถามทาง (How to get there) — page 177

❷ ในโรงแรม (At a hotel) — page 179

❸ ในภัตตาคาร (In a restaurant) — page 181

❹ ที่ธนาคาร (At a bank) — page 189

❺ ที่สถานีตำรวจ (At a police station) — page 191

❻ ไปหาหมอ (At a medical doctor) — page 195

❼ โทรศัพท์และไปรษณีย์ (Telephone and post) — page 199

❽ การขนส่งมวลชน (Public transportation) — page 203

❾ การซื้อของและการต่อรองราคา (Shopping and bargaining) — page 209

การถามทาง
(How to get there)

Useful expressions:

ทิศ , ทาง	direction
เดินไปตาม	walk along
ตรงไป	straight on
ทางซ้าย	left, on the left side
ทางขวา	right, on the right side
ทางเหนือ	northward
ทางใต้	southward
ข้างบน	up
ข้างล่าง	down
ข้างหน้า	in front
ข้างหลัง	behind
ข้างใน	inside
ข้างนอก	outside
เลี้ยว	turn
ข้าม	cross
ขึ้น	walk up
ลง	walk down
เข้า	walk in
ออก	walk out

บทสนทนา ❶

ทอม	ขอโทษครับ ห้องน้ำอยู่ที่ไหนครับ	Excuse me, where is the toilet, please?
ทิพย์	อยู่ที่ชั้นบนค่ะ คุณขึ้นบันไดไป แล้วเลี้ยวซ้ายนะคะ ห้องน้ำชายอยู่ทางขวาค่ะ	It is in the next floor. You walk up the staircase, then turn left. The Gentleman's toilet is on the right side.
ทอม	ขอบคุณครับ	Thank you.

บทสนทนา ❷

ทอม	ขอโทษครับ หอการค้าไทย - เยอรมันอยู่ที่ไหนครับ	Excuse me please, where is the Thai - German Chamber of Commerce?
ทิพย์	อยู่ที่อาคารกองบุญมา ชั้น 6 ถนนสีลม เฉียงๆกับโรงแรมนารายณ์ค่ะ	It is in the 6 th. floor of Gongbunma building on Silom street, almost opposite Narai Hotels.

ในโรงแรม
(At a hotel)

In Thailand many kinds of accommodation are available, starting from very cheap one to very expensive one. The price is generally quoted per room and excludes breakfast. It is possible that small hotels and pensions charge you more on weekend than on a **weekday** whereas at first and luxury class hotels it is normally more expensive during the high **season** (November until April) than during the low season.

A double room (ห้องคู่) has 2 separate small beds (เตียงเดี่ยว). Small hotels and pensions do not charge for service and tax, contrary to first and luxury class hotels. The latter have air conditioned rooms only whereas tourist class hotels provide both rooms with air conditioner and with fan. In a hotel, the bathroom is within the bedroom; in pensions it might be that the bathroom is externally located. Check-in and check-out time is normally 12 a.m.

บทสนทนา ❶

ดอริส	มีห้องว่างไหมคะ	Do you have a vacant room?
พนักงาน	มีแต่ห้องแอร์ครับ ห้องพัดลมเต็มหมด	Only air conditioned rooms are free. All rooms with fan are full.
ดอริส	ค่าห้องวันละเท่าไรคะ	How much is it per day?
พนักงาน	ห้องเดี่ยววันละ 350 บาท ห้องคู่วันละ 450 บาทครับ	Single room is 350 Baht per day, double room 450 Baht.

	ถ้าคุณพัก 1 สัปดาห์ขึ้นไป เราลด 10 เปอร์เซ็นต์ คุณจะพักกี่วันครับ	In case you stay 1 week or longer we will give you a 10 % discount. How long do you like to stay?
ดอริส	ยังไม่ทราบค่ะ ดิฉันขอดูห้องก่อนได้ไหมคะ	I do not know yet. Could I see the room, please?
พนักงาน	ได้ครับ เชิญทางนี้ครับ	Of course. This way, please.

บทสนทนา ❷

ดอริส	ขอโทษค่ะ ขอฝากของไว้ที่นี่ได้ไหมคะ	Excuse me, please. Could I deposit my belongings here?
พนักงาน	ได้ครับ มีอะไรบ้างครับ	Yes, what is it?
ดอริส	มีกล้องถ่ายรูปกับหนังสือเดินทางค่ะ	It is a photo camera and a passport.
พนักงาน	นี่ใบรับฝากและรายการสิ่งของ ช่วยเซ็นต์ชื่อตรงนี้ด้วยครับ	Here is your receipt with a list of all things. Please sign here.
ดอริส	ขอบคุณ	Thank you.

ในภัตตาคาร
(In a restaurant)

For Thais it is a great entertainment and fun to eat out and there are restaurants at everyone's reach. Your main decision when you eat out is whether you choose to eat one dish just for yourself (อาหารจานเดียว) or whether you order just a dish of plain rice and eat all dishes with your friends. A basic rule for the composition of a meal for more than 1 person is to select for every dish a contrasting one, e.g. a spicy hot one you choose combining with a mild one, a salty or a sour one with a soup, ... Almost everything is eaten with folk and spoon; the right hand will hold the spoon. People usually eat noodle soup with chopsticks and a spoon. Knifes are not used at all as everything you eat has been cut to mouthpieces before or you can easily use the folk to make it smaller. Some restaurants offer for each dish an additional spoon which you use to transport the food to your own plain rice dish; in addition to this you may be served a small bowl with spoon for the soup you ordered. In the case you do not get it, just take the soup from the "big pot or bowl" with your own spoon.

บทสนทนา ❶

ดอริส	ขอเมนูภาษาอังกฤษหน่อยค่ะ	Could I have the English menu, please?
บริกร	นี่ครับ สั่งอะไรดีครับ	Here it is. What do you like to order?
ดอริส	ขอน้ำส้มคั้น 2 แก้วก่อนค่ะ ที่นี่มีอะไรอร่อยคะ	At first we would like to have 2 glasses of orange juice. What is your speciality here?

บริกร	ต้มยำกุ้ง ทอดมันปลากราย และห่อหมกครับ	Dtoom Yam Gung, Todman Bplagrai and Homook.
ดอริส	ขอต้มยำกุ้ง ไม่เผ็ดมากนะคะ ทอดมัน ผัดผักรวม และข้าว ด้วยค่ะ	We would like to have Dtoom Yum Gung, but not too spicy, Todman, Pat Pak Ruam and also rice.
บริกร	ครับ	Yes.
ดอริส	เก็บเงินด้วยค่ะ	Check bill, please.
บริกร	290 บาทครับ	290 Baht.

Useful expressions:

หิวไหม	Are you hungry?
หิวน้ำไหม	Are you thirsty?
กินข้าวแล้วหรือยัง	Have you already eaten?
ทานอาหารไทยเป็นไหม	Can you eat Thai food?
ชอบทานอาหารไทยไหม	Do you like Thai food?
ทานอาหารเผ็ดได้ไหม	Can you eat spicy dishes?
ไม่เอาเผ็ดมากนะ	I do not like it too spicy.
ผมทานเจ , ผมทานมังสะวิรัติ	I am vegetarian.
มี........ไหม	Do you have ....?
นี่ไม่ได้สั่ง	I did not order this.
ใส่.......	with ....

ไม่ใส่.......	without ....
รับประทาน , ทาน , กิน	eat

Useful words concerning with eating:

เครื่องดื่ม (beverage):

ชา	tea
กาแฟ	coffee
น้ำเปล่า , น้ำดื่ม	drinking water (not mineral water)
น้ำเย็น	cold water
น้ำแข็งเปล่า	ice water
น้ำแข็ง	ice
นม(สด)	milk
โกโก้	cocoa
น้ำส้มคั้น	orange juice
น้ำมะนาว	lemon juice
เบียร์	beer
เหล้า	whisky
ดื่ม	drink

เครื่องปรุงรส (spices):

น้ำตาล	sugar
เกลือ	salt
พริกไทย	pepper
น้ำปลา	fish sauce

พริก	chilli
พริกป่น	chilli powder
น้ำส้ม	vinegar
มะนาว	lime

อาหารประเภทข้าว (rice dishes):

ข้าวเปล่า , ข้าวสวย	plain rice
ข้าวต้ม	plain rice soup
ข้าวเหนียว	sticky rice
ข้าวผัด.......	fried rice with ....
ข้าวต้ม.......	rice soup with ....
เนื้อ(วัว)	cow meat
หมู	pork meat
ไก่	poultry
กุ้ง	shrimp, prawn
ปู	crab
หอย	shell, oyster
ปลาหมึก	squid
เป็ด	duck

อาหารประเภทก๋วยเตี๋ยว (noodle dishes):

ก๋วยเตี๋ยว	rice noodle
เส้นใหญ่	wide rice noodle
เส้นเล็ก	thin rice noodle
เส้นหมี่	vermicelli rice noodle

บะหมี่	egg noodle
ก๋วยเตี๋ยว........แห้ง	dry rice noodle with ...
ก๋วยเตี๋ยว........น้ำ	rice noodle soup with ...
ผัดซีอิ๊ว	fried rice noodle with soya souse
ก๋วยเตี๋ยวราดหน้า	fried rice noodle with gravy
ลูกชิ้น	meat ball (cow, pork, fish, shrimp)
หมูแดง	grilled pork meat
หมูสับ	minced pork meat

อาหารประเภทไข่ (egg dish):

ไข่ลวก	soft boiled egg
ไข่ต้ม	hard boiled egg
ไข่ดาว	fried egg
ไข่เจียว	omelette

อาหารจานโปรด (popular dishes):

แกงจืด......	clear soup with ....
แกง(เผ็ด).......	curry with ....
ต้มยำ......	spicy sour soup with ....
ต้มข่าไก่	spicy sour coconut milk soup with poultry
แกงส้ม......	Curry with fish or shrimp and vegetable (without coconut milk)

ยำ......	Thai salad (spicy) with ......
ผัด.....	fried ....
ผัดเผ็ด.......	fried (spicy) ....
........ทอดกระเทียมพริกไทย	fried (with garlic and pepper) ...
........เผา , ปิ้ง , ย่าง	grilled ....
........ทอด	deep fried ....
........นึ่ง	steamed ....
........ยัดไส้	filled ....
........อบ	backed ....
........หม้อดิน	..... in the chicken brick

ผัก (vegetable):

ผัก	vegetable
หน่อไม้	young bamboo
กระเพรา	basil
ดอกกระหล่ำ	cauliflower
ถั่ว	bean
ถั่วลันเตา	pea
แตงกวา	cucumber
ขิง	ginger
กระเทียม	garlic
กระหล่ำปลี	cabbage
ผักชี	coriander
เห็ด	mushroom

หน่อไม้ฝรั่ง	asparagus
มะเขือเทศ	tomato
หอมใหญ่	onion
ต้นหอม	spring onion

ผลไม้ (fruit):

ผลไม้	fruit
สับปะรด	pineapple
กล้วย	banana
ฝรั่ง	guava
มะพร้าว	coconut
มะม่วง	mango
มังคุด	mangosteen
ส้มโอ	pomelo
มะละกอ	papaya
ส้ม	orange, mandarin
เงาะ	rambutan
แตงไทย	melon
องุ่น	grape
แตงโม	watermelon

อุปกรณ์การรับประทาน (eating instruments):

ร้านอาหาร , ภัตตาคาร	restaurant

เมนู , รายการอาหาร	menu
จาน	dish
ชาม	bowl
ถ้วย	cup, small bowl
แก้ว	glass
ช้อน	spoon
ส้อม	folk
มีด	knife
ตะเกียบ	chopsticks
ขวด	bottle
ที่เขี่ยบุหรี่	ash tray

ที่ธนาคาร
(At a bank)

The basic denomination of the Thai currency is **บาท**. It is divided in 100 **สตางค์**. Well known credit cards are accepted in hotels, restaurants, shopping malls, supermarkets, bookstores, Jewellery shops, boutiques, etc. in Bangkok and all other big cities.

Banks are at present in every district in Thailand though not all offer Foreign Exchange. Generally this service is only available in cities or touristic areas. Opening hours for Thai banks are weekdays from 8.30 a.m. to 3.30 p.m.; on weekends, holidays, and bank holidays banks are closed. A few banks offer an external Foreign Exchange Service (outside of the branch) which opens seven days a week until 6 p.m. or 8 p.m. (varying from branch to branch).

In addition it is possible to do Foreign Exchange in large hotels or authorised money changers (sometimes 24 hours a day), yet the rate you receive is in general not as good as the one banks offer.

บทสนทนา ❶

ดอริส	ดิฉันขอแลกเช็คเดินทางหน่อยค่ะ	I would like to change some travellers cheques please.
พนักงาน	ขอหนังสือเดินทางด้วยค่ะ	May I see your passport, please?

ดอริส	อัตราแลกเปลี่ยนของวันนี้เท่าไรคะ	What is the rate today?
พนักงาน	24.35 บาทต่อ 1 ดอลลาร์ค่ะ	24.35 Baht for one Dollar.
	ช่วยเซ็นต์ชื่อตรงนี้หน่อยนะคะ	Please sign your name here.
ดอริส	ขอบคุณค่ะ	Thank you.

ที่สถานีตำรวจ
(At a police station)

Should any of your belongings vanish from your hotel room, please contact the manager first. He will tell you whether you should contact the police or not.

If you happen to be the victim of a pickpocket, please do not try to get your stolen things back yourself but inform the next police station and if possible ask for an English speaking officer. Tell your story in a clear and easy English. In Bangkok and other large touristic towns an English speaking tourist police is available. In small towns it is quite difficult to find someone being able to speak a language other than Thai.

Useful vocabulary and idioms

ผมถูกขโมยเงิน	My money has been stolen.
.......ของผมหาย	My ...... disappeared.
ตำรวจ	police
ตำรวจท่องเที่ยว	tourist police
สถานีตำรวจ	police station
มีอุบัติเหตุเกิดขึ้นที่......	An accident took place in ....
ขโมย	thief, to steal

Warnings and calls for help

ช่วยด้วย!	Help!

ไฟไหม้!	fire!
ขโมย!	thief!
ระวัง!	watch out!
ตำรวจ!	police!

บทสนทนา ❶

ตำรวจ	สวัสดีครับ คุณมีปัญหาอะไรครับ	Hello, what happened?
จอห์น	ผมถูกขโมย	I was robbed.
ตำรวจ	มีอะไรหายบ้างครับ	What did you lose?
จอห์น	กล้องนิคอน เอฟ 501 ติดเลนส์ นิคอร์ 35 - 135 หนังสือเดินทาง บัตรอเมริกันเอ็กซ์เพรส และเงินสดประมาณ 2000 บาทครับ	A Nikon F501 with a 35 to 135 mm Nikkor lens, a passport, an American Express credit card and about 2000 Baht in cash.
ตำรวจ	หายที่ไหนครับ	Where did you lose them?
จอห์น	ผมวางกระเป๋าไว้บนหาดทราย ตอนผมไปว่ายน้ำครับ	I left my bag on the beach when I went for a swim.
ตำรวจ	อย่างนี้คงหาตัวขโมยยากหน่อย	In this case, it is going to be difficult to find the thief.
	แต่เราก็จะพยายามนะครับ คุณจะอยู่ในเมืองไทยอีกกี่วัน	Anyway we will try. How long will you stay in Thailand?

	เราจะติดต่อคุณได้ที่ไหนครับ	Where can we contact you?
จอห์น	ผมพักที่โรงแรมโซฟิเทลถึงวันที่ 15 เดือนนี้ครับ	I stay in Sofitel Hotel until the 15th of this month.

ไปหาหมอ
(At a medical doctor)

It is advisable to buy a health insurance for abroad, as the cost might be very high in case of a treatment of an injury or illness. In case of an illness you can go to private clinics or hospitals. For not very serious problems you can buy the medicine without prescription at a pharmacy.

Useful vocabulary and idioms

ผมจะไปหาหมอได้ที่ไหน	Where can I visit a medical doctor?
ร้านขายยาอยู่ที่ไหน	Where can I find a pharmacy?
ผมแพ้......	I am allergic to ....
มียาแก้.....ไหม	What do you have against ......?
ยานี้ใช้อย่างไร	How do I use this medicine?
มีปัญหาอะไร , เป็นอะไร	What happened? What is the problem?
ผมเป็นไข้	I have got a fever.
ผมไอ	I have got a cough.
ผมถูกแดดเผา	I am sunburned.
ผมปวดท้อง	I have stomachache.
ผมปวดฟัน	I have toothache.
ผมถูกหมากัด	I was bitten by a dog.

ผมถูกแมลงต่อย	I was bitten by an insect.
คุณไม่เป็นอะไรมาก	It is not serious.
ยา(กิน)	medicine (to take)
ยาทา	medical cream
คุณต้องนอนพัก	You have to stay in bed.
คนไข้	patient
พยาบาล	nurse
หมอ , แพทย์	medical doctor
หมอฟัน , ทันตแพทย์	dentist
โรงพยาบาล	hospital
ร้านหมอ	private clinic
ร้านขายยา	pharmacy
เภสัชกร	pharmacist
ผมรู้สึกเจ็บที่นี่	I have got pain here.
เลือด	blood
ผ้าพันแผล	bandage
ยาแก้ปวด	painkiller
ผมหายใจไม่ออก	I can not breathe.
ผมนอนไม่หลับ	I can not sleep.
คัน	itch
เป็นลม	dizzy
แผล , บาดแผล	wound, cut
รถพยาบาล	ambulance
โรค	illness, disease

บทสนทนา ❶ (ที่ร้านขายยา)

วิลเลียม	มียาแก้หวัดไหมครับ	Do you have something against the cold?
เภสัชกร	เป็นไข้หรือเปล่า ตัวร้อนไหมครับ	Have you got a fever, is your temperature high?
วิลเลียม	ไม่ครับ แต่ผมไอ เจ็บคอ และปวดศีรษะด้วย	No but I have got a cough, a soar throat, and headache.
เภสัชกร	คุณทานยานี้ครั้งละ 2 เม็ด สามเวลาหลังอาหารและก่อนนอนนะครับ แล้วยาแก้ไอนี่คุณจิบบ่อยๆหรือเวลารู้สึกเจ็บคอ คุณต้องนอนมากๆและอย่าดื่มน้ำเย็น อย่าถูกแดดนะครับ	Take 2 pills each time, 3 times after meal and also before you go to bed everyday, take the cough mixture several times or when you feel soar in your throat. Your must remain in bed and are not allowed to drink cold water; do not go out in the sun.
วิลเลียม	ครับ ทั้งหมดเท่าไรครับ	OK, how much is it all together?
เภสัชกร	260 บาท	260 Baht.

บทสนทนา ❷

หมอ	สวัสดีครับ คุณเป็นอะไรครับ	Hello, what is the problem?
คนไข้	สวัสดีค่ะ ดิฉันรู้สึกไม่สบายค่ะ	Hello, I feel sick.
หมอ	อาการเป็นอย่างไรครับ	What is your symptom?

คนไข้	ดิฉันท้องเสียบ่อยๆค่ะ บางครั้งอาเจียนด้วย	I have often got a diarrhoea. Up and now I also have to vomit.
หมอ	คุณอยู่เมืองไทยมานานแล้วหรือยังครับ	How long have you been in Thailand?
คนไข้	ประมาณ 10 วันค่ะ	About 10 days.
หมอ	คุณอาจจะไม่เคยชินกับอาหารไทย คุณรับประทานยานี้ครั้งละ 1 เม็ดทุก 4 ชั่วโมง และอย่ารับประทานอาหารรสจัดนะครับ	Maybe you are not yet used to the Thai cuisine. Take this medicine. One pill every 4 hours. Do not eat too spicy food!
คนไข้	ขอบคุณค่ะ	Thank you.

โทรศัพท์และไปรษณีย์
(Telephone and Post)

There are telephone boxes at almost every place. You need either 1 or 5 Baht coins or a telephone card. More and more mobile telephone stations are available.

By the way, if you want to look up some number in the English telephone directory you first have to look for the first name which is followed by the family name and not the family name first.

Normally you can have your overseas calls done at post offices. The cost hereof and the possibility of collect calls are subject to the contracts between การสื่อสารแห่งประเทศไทย" (Masscommunication Authority of Thailand) and the target countries. Minimum 3 minutes are required. "โทรแบบไม่เจาะจงตัว" (a Station Call) is cheaper than "โทรแบบเจาะจงตัว" (a Personal call).

บทสนทนา ❶

เควิน	สวัสดีครับ	Hello.
	ผมโทรจากห้อง 302 ช่วยต่อ	I call from room no. 302.
	ตำรวจท่องเที่ยวหน่อยครับ	Could you please connect me with the tourist police?
พนักงาน	ค่ะ	Yes.
	สายไม่ว่างค่ะ	The line is busy.
	ถือสายรอนะคะ	Please wait.

	ฮัลโหล ไม่มีใครรับสายค่ะ	Hello .... no one answers.
เควิน	ไม่เป็นไรครับ	It does not a matter.
	ขอบคุณครับ	Thank you.

บทสนทนา ❷

เอลเลน	สวัสดีค่ะ ขอพูดกับคุณทิพย์วรรณหน่อยค่ะ	Hello, could I talk to Khun Tipawan, please?
คุณแม่	รอเดี๋ยวนะคะ	Wait for a moment, please.
	เขาไม่อยู่ค่ะ	She is not in.
เอลเลน	ขอโทษค่ะ คุณทิพย์วรรณจะกลับเมื่อไรคะ	Excuse me, please. At what time will Khun Tipawan be back?
คุณแม่	ไม่ทราบค่ะ เขาไม่ได้บอกไว้ คุณจะสั่งอะไรไว้ไหมคะ	I do not know, she did not tell me. Do you like to leave a message for her?
เอลเลน	ช่วยบอกว่า เอลเลนโทรมานะคะ	Just tell her that Ellen called.
คุณแม่	จะให้เขาโทรกลับไหมคะ	Do you like her to call you back?
เอลเลน	ไม่ต้องค่ะ ดิฉันจะโทรมาใหม่ตอนค่ำๆ ขอบคุณค่ะ สวัสดีค่ะ	No need, I will call her once again in the evening. Thank you. Bye.
คุณแม่	สวัสดีค่ะ	Bye.

When the Thai receive a telephone call, they will not answer by saying their name but just indicating the place (for business calls) or telephone number (private calls).

บทสนทนา ❸ (ในที่ทำการไปรษณีย์)

ริชาร์ด	ผมขอโทรไปสหรัฐ สามนาที ไม่เจาะจงตัวครับ	I would like to phone up the U.S.A. I want to have a station call for 3 minutes.
เจ้า - หน้าที่	ขอรหัสเมืองกับเบอร์โทรศัพท์ ด้วยครับ	Could you please give me the area code and the number?
ริชาร์ด	รหัส 0221 เบอร์โทรศัพท์ 485953	0221-485953
จ.	ชื่อผู้พูดครับ	Your name, please?
ริชาร์ด	ริชาร์ด บริดจ์	Richard Bridge.
เจ้า - หน้าที่	คอยสักครู่ ตู้สองครับ	Please wait for a moment. The second box, please.

At the post office:

The opening times for post offices in Thailand is from 8.00 a.m. till 4.00 p.m. during weekdays and before noon on weekends. The mail is delivered twice a day - once at weekends.

บทสนทนา ❹ (ในที่ทำการไปรษณีย์)

โรเจอร์	ผมต้องการส่งพัสดุห่อนี้ไป อังกฤษครับ	I would like to send this parcel to England.

จ.	ทางอากาศหรือทางเรือครับ	Via airmail or surface mail?
โรเจอร์	ทางเรือครับ เมื่อไรถึงครับ	Via surface mail. How long does it take?
จ.	ประมาณ 2 เดือนครับ	About 2 months.
โรเจอร์	ผมมีจดหมายและไปรษณี-ยบัตรด้วย จะส่งทางอากาศครับ	I also have some letters and postcards which I want to send by airmail.
จ.	จดหมายลงทะเบียนหรือเปล่าครับ	Do you want to send the letters registered?
โรเจอร์	ไม่ต้องครับ	No.
	ผมขอซื้อแสตมป์ 2 บาท 3 ดวง แอโรแกรม 4 ฉบับและซองจดหมาย 3 ซองด้วยครับ ทั้งหมดเท่าไรครับ	I also would like to buy 3 x 2 Baht stamps, 4 aerogramms and 3 envelopes. How much is it all-together?
จ.	732 บาท	732 Baht.

การขนส่งมวลชน
(Public transportation)

By bus:

Within Bangkok

There are 2 kinds of buses, the normal one (not air-conditioned) and the air-conditioned buses. During the rush hours from 7 a.m. to 9 a.m. and 4 p.m. to 7 p.m. all buses are normally completely full.

บทสนทนา ❶

บิล	ขอโทษครับ ผมจะไปประตูน้ำ ผมจะต้องขึ้นรถสายอะไรครับ	Excuse me, please. I would like to go to Bpradtunam. Which bus do I have to take?
ทิพย์	สาย 2 หรือสาย 60 ก็ได้ค่ะ	Line 2 or 60.
บิล	ขอบคุณครับ	Thank you.

บทสนทนา ❷ (ในรถประจำทาง)

บิล	ขอโทษครับ อีกไกลไหมครับ กว่าจะถึงประตูน้ำ	Excuse me, please. Is it still far until we reach Bpradtunam?
ทิพย์	ไม่ไกลค่ะ อีก 2 - 3 ป้าย เท่านั้น	No, just 2 or 3 more stops.
บิล	พอถึงแล้ว คุณช่วยบอกผม	When we reach it, could you please

	หน่อยได้ไหมครับ	tell me?
ทิพย์	ได้ค่ะ	Yes.
	ป้ายหน้า คุณลงได้แล้วค่ะ	You can get of at the next bus-stop.
บิล	ขอบคุณมากครับ	Thank you very much.

By bus:

Between cities

Bangkok is the main bus centre to places all over the country. The "southern bus terminal" (สถานีขนส่งสายใต้) is located at the Bpinglao-Nakonshaisi road. The "northern (สถานีขนส่งสายเหนือ) and the north eastern (สถานีขนส่งสายตะวันออกเฉียงเหนือ) bus terminals" are on Pahoonyootin road (หมอชิต). Last but not least the "eastern bus terminal" (สถานีขนส่งสายตะวันออก) is located on Sukumwit road (เอกมัย).

There are 3 kinds of buses:

- normal orange buses   รถธรรมดา , รถพัดลม
- air-conditioned buses   รถปรับอากาศ , รถทัวร์ , รถแอร์
- VIP air-conditioned buses รถนอนพิเศษ ,รถวีไอพี

Normal orange buses with fan are fairly cheap, though no reservation can be made and the buses do have quite many stops.

Air-conditioned buses normally go non-stop to the destination. For a long journey it is advisable to take a VIP air-conditioned bus. Of course it is more expensive but much more comfortable. You are advised to pre-book for weekends or holidays.

บทสนทนา ❸

ดอริส	ขอโทษค่ะ ดิฉันจะไปเกาะสมุย ซื้อตั๋วได้ที่ไหนคะ	Excuse me please, I would like to go to Ko Samui. Where can I buy the ticket?
ไทย	ช่อง 4 ตรงโน้นครับ	Counter 4, overt here.
ดอริส	ขอบคุณค่ะ	Thank you.
ดอริส	ตั๋วไปเกาะสมุย 2 ใบค่ะ ขอด้านซ้ายตรงกลางรถนะคะ รถออกกี่โมงคะ	Two tickets to Ko Samui, please. I would like to have the seats on the left side, in the middle of the bus. At what time does the bus depart?
ผู้ขาย	สี่ทุ่มค่ะ ชานชาลา 9 นะคะ	At 10 p.m. Platform number 9.

Taxi and Tuk-Tuk:

Most taxis are equipped with meter. For those which lack this equipment, you have to bargain which can be of some fun. For Tuk-Tuk's you always have to bargain. Be aware that they hardly accept rides longer than about 5 kilometres. Both, Taxis and Tuk-Tuk normally do not belong to the driver. Therefore during 4 and 5 p.m. it is quite difficult to get a taxi as it is the time for the driver to give the car back to the garage.

บทสนทนา ❹

ฮันส์	ไปสถานทูตเยอรมันที่ถนนสาธรใต้ เท่าไรครับ	To the German embassy at the Saton Dtai road; how much does it cost?
คนขับ	60 บาทครับ	60 Baht.
ฮันส์	แพงเกินไป 50 บาทได้ไหมครับ	Too expensive. 50 Baht, o.k?
คนขับ	ขออีก 5 บาทนะครับ	Could I have 5 Baht more?
ฮันส์	ตกลง	O.K.

บทสนทนา ❺

มาเทียส	ไปซอยงามดูพลี เท่าไรครับ	Tuk-Tuk, how much is it to the Ngam Du Pli lane?
ตุ๊ก ตุ๊ก	เข้าซอยไกลไหม	Do I have to drive far inside the lane?
มาเทียส	ประมาณ 500 เมตร	About 500 meter.
ตุ๊ก ตุ๊ก	40 บาทครับ	40 Baht
มาเทียส	เลี้ยวซ้ายแล้วตรงไป ขับช้าๆ หน่อยได้ไหม จอดตรงนี้ครับ	Turn left and then straight on. Please drive a bit slower. Could you stop here, please?

By train:

There are 3 classes in the train. The price of the 3 rd. class is about the same as the normal orange bus. The place can either not be reserved in advance. It is not recommended to use this way of transport for a long journey. The 2 nd. class train has both sitting and sleeping cars with fan or air-conditioners. The price is roughly the same as in air-conditioned buses. The first class is rather expensive. There are single and double beds available.

You can buy a train ticket up to **3 months in advance.**

On some routes, combined tickets of train, ship, and hotel are available.

บทสนทนา ๖

รอย	เชียงใหม่ ตอนเย็นพรุ่งนี้ รถด่วนพิเศษ ชั้น 2 นอน เตียงบน พัดลมครับ	Chiangmai, tomorrow evening, special express, 2 nd. class, upper bed with fan, please.
พนักงาน	คนเดียวใช่ไหมครับ	For one person?
รอย	ครับ รถออกกี่โมงครับ	Yes, when does the train depart?
พนักงาน	ทุ่มสิบห้า ชานชาลา 3 ครับ	7.15 p.m., platform 3.
รอย	แล้วถึงเชียงใหม่กี่โมงครับ	When will we reach Chiangmai?
พนักงาน	เจ็ดโมง สี่สิบห้า	At 7.45 a.m.

By ship and plane:

In general one can not use a boat or ship very often; but in Bangkok it is quite a good idea to cross the Chao Phrya river by ferry in order to avoid the notorious traffic congestion.

Express boats along the Chao Phrya river from Bangkok to Nonburi are the most inexpensive, though not very comfortable, way to discover an original Thai way of life.

You can travel by ship to some tourist attractions like Ayudhya, Hua Hin, Pattaya, Samui, Songkhla or even Chiangmai, but you have to book in a travel agency and it is rather expensive.

Domestic flights are **good** for tourists who do not have much time and want to travel comfortably, yet much of the landscape can not be seen at all.

การซื้อของและการต่อรองราคา
(Shopping and bargaining)

Thailand is a very good and cheap place to shop. Good bargains are cotton-fabric, silk, jewellery, handicrafts, shoes, clothes, decoration items, ... In shopping centres, prices are fixed. But in markets, small shops and with vendors it is possible and fun to bargain.

To take Statues of Buddha or antiques out of the country needs permission from the "Department of Fine Arts" of the ministry of Education.

Useful vocabularies and expressions:

........อยู่ที่ไหน	Where is.......?
ร้านขาย.......อยู่ที่ไหน	Where is........-shop?
ซื้อ.......ได้ที่ไหน	Where can I buy ......?
ผมต้องการ........	I would like to ......
มี......ไหม	Do you have ...? Are there.....?
ขอดู........ได้ไหม	Can I see the ......?
มีแบบอื่นไหม	Do you have other patterns?
ขอลองได้ไหม	Can I try it?
ราคาเท่าไร	How much is it?

ลด(ราคา)หน่อยได้ไหม	Can you reduce the price a bit?
มีถูกกว่านี้ไหม	Do you have something cheaper?
ขอ......บาทได้ไหม	Can I get it for …… Baht?
ถูกที่สุดได้เท่าไร	What is the cheapest price?
เล็ก / เล็กไป	small / too small
ใหญ่ / ใหญ่ไป	big / too big
ยาว / ยาวไป	long / too long
สั้น / สั้นไป	short / too short
คับ / คับไป	tight / too tight
กว้าง / กว้างไป	wide / too wide
หนา / หนาไป	thick / too thick
บาง / บางไป	thin / too thin
แพง / แพงไป	expensive / too expensive
ถูก	cheap
ขอใบเสร็จด้วย	I would like to have a receipt.
กิโลละ.......บาท	..... Baht per kilo.
เมตรละ......บาท	..... Baht per meter.
โหลละ.......บาท	..... Baht per dozen.
........บาท ขาดตัว	..... Baht, the lowest price.
ไม่ได้ ขาดทุน	..... no, this is lower than my cost.
ร้านขายรองเท้า	shoe shop
ร้านขายหนังสือ	book shop
ร้านขายเสื้อผ้า	clothes shop
ร้านตัดผม	hairdresser

ร้านเสริมสวย	beauty salon
ร้านตัดเสื้อผู้ชาย	tailor
ร้านตัดเสื้อผู้หญิง	dressmaker
ตลาด	market
ซุปเปอร์มาร์เก็ต	supermarket
ห้างสรรพสินค้า	shopping centre
ซื้อ	buy
ขาย	sell
ผู้ซื้อ, ลูกค้า	customer
ผู้ขาย, พ่อค้า, แม่ค้า	seller

Personal hygiene products:

ครีมกันแดด	sun cream
สบู่	soap
แชมพู	shampoo
ยาสีฟัน	toothpaste
แปรงสีฟัน	toothbrush
ใบมีดโกน	razor blade
ครีมโกนหนวด	razor cream
หวี	comb
กระดาษชำระ	toilet paper
ผ้าอนามัย	sanitary napkins

Clothes:

กางเกงยีนส์	jeans
กางเกงใน	underwear
กางเกงขาสั้น	shorts
กางเกงขายาว	trousers
กระโปรง	skirt
กระโปรงชุด	costume
เสื้อ	shirt, blouse
เสื้อชั้นใน	brassièr
เสื้อยืด	T-shirt
เสื้อแขนสั้น	short sleeved shirt
เสื้อแขนยาว	long sleeved shirt
ถุงเท้า	socks
รองเท้า	shoes
รองเท้าแตะ	slippers
ชุดอาบน้ำ	swim suit
เข็มขัด	belt
ผ้าเช็ดตัว	towel
ผ้าเช็ดหน้า	handkerchief
ผ้าฝ้าย	cotton
ผ้าไหม	silk
ผ้าตัดเสื้อ	fabric for clothes
ชุดสูท	suit

เสื้อนอก	jacket
หมวก	hat

Miscellaneous:

ปากกา	pen
ดินสอ	pencil
กระดาษ	paper
แผนที่	map
ฟิล์มสี	negative film
ฟิล์มสไลด์	slide film
แว่นตา	glasses
แว่นกันแดด	sun glasses
นาฬิกา	watch
ยากันยุง	insect repellent
ผงซักฟอก	detergent
น้ำยาล้างจาน	dish washing **detergent**
กระเป๋าสตางค์	wallet
สร้อยข้อมือ	wristlet
สร้อยคอ	necklace
แหวน	ring
ทอง	gold
เงิน	silver
ทองเหลือง	bronze
เพชร	diamond

ทับทิม	ruby
มรกต	emerald
ไพลิน	sapphire
หยก	jade
ของที่ระลึก	souvenir

Colours:

สี	colour
ขาว	white
ครีม	beige
เหลือง	yellow
ส้ม	orange
แดง	red
ชมพู	pink
ฟ้า	light blue
น้ำเงิน	blue
ม่วง	violet
เขียว	green
น้ำตาล	brown
เทา	grey
ดำ	black
อ่อน	light
แก่	dark

บทสนทนา

ผู้ซื้อ	ขอดูเสื้อเชิ้ตหน่อยครับ	Can I see a shirt?
ผู้ขาย	ตัวไหนคะ	Which one?
ผู้ซื้อ	ตัวสีขาวครับ	The white one.
ผู้ขาย	นี่ผ้าไหมแท้นะคะ เนื้อดีมาก	It is genuine silk. Very good quality.
ผู้ซื้อ	ตัวละเท่าไรครับ	How much is it?
ผู้ขาย	450 บาทค่ะ	450 Baht.
ผู้ซื้อ	แพงไป ลดหน่อยได้ไหมครับ	Too expensive. Can you make it a bit cheaper?
ผู้ขาย	ให้เท่าไรคะ	How much do you want to pay?
ผู้ซื้อ	300 ถ้วนนะครับ	Exactly 300.
ผู้ขาย	ไม่ได้ค่ะ ขาดทุน 400 ก็แล้วกันนะคะ	No, this is cheaper than what I paid for it. 400, O.K.?
ผู้ซื้อ	แพงไป ลดอีกหน่อยไม่ได้หรือครับ	Too expensive. Can't you make it a bit cheaper?
ผู้ขาย	380 บาทขาดตัวค่ะ นี่ถูกที่สุดแล้ว รับกี่ตัวคะ	380 is the lowest price. This is the cheapest. How many do you like to have?
ผู้ซื้อ	ตัวเดียวครับ	Only one.

About the author

Tipawan Thampusana-Abold was born in Bangkok. After finishing the "Triam Udom Suksa High School", she studied at the Faculty of Arts, Chulalongkorn University "Thai" (as major subject) as well as "English and history" (as minor subjects) and was graduated with "Bachelor of Arts". Afterwards she studied at the same University "Non-Formal-Education" and was graduated with "Master of Education".

Until she moved to Germany in 1990, Tipawan Thampusana-Abold worked as a teacher for Thai and English, a tourism development officer, and a freelance writer.

At the moment she lives in Augsburg, Germany and works as a freelance writer and photographer as well as a teacher for Thai language.